Preface

This student revision aid is based on the principle that in any close examination of Shakespeare's plays 'the text's the thing'. Seeing a performance, or listening to a tape or record of a performance, is essential and is in itself a valuable and stimulating experience in understanding and appreciation. However, a real evaluation of Shakespeare's greatness, of his universality and of the nature of his literary and dramatic art, can only be achieved by constant application to the texts of the plays themselves. These revised editions of Brodie's Notes are intended to supplement that process through detailed critical commentary.

The first aim of each book is to fix the whole play in the reader's mind by providing a concise summary of the plot, relating it back, where appropriate, to its source or sources. Subsequently the book provides a summary of each scene, followed by *critical comments*. These may convey its importance in the dramatic structure of the play, creation of atmosphere, indication of character development, significance of figurative language etc, and they will also explain or paraphrase difficult words or phrases and identify meaningful references. At the end of each act revision questions are set to test the student's specific and broad understanding and appreciation of the play.

An extended critical commentary follows this scene by scene analysis. This embraces such major elements as characterization, imagery, the use of blank verse and prose, soliloquies and other aspects of the play which the editor considers need close attention. The paramount aim is to send the reader back to the text. The book concludes with a series of revision questions which require a detailed knowledge of the play; the first of these has notes by the editor of what *might* be included in a written answer. The intention is to stimulate and to guide; the whole emphasis of this commentary is to encourage the student's *involvement* in the play, to develop disciplined critical responses and thus promote personal enrichment through the imaginative experience of our greatest writer.

Graham Handley

Contents

DISCARDED

Line references in these Notes are to the
Arden Shakespeare: As You Like It,
but as references are also given
to particular acts and scenes,
the Notes may be used
with any edition of the play.

Shakespeare and the Elizabethan playhouse

William Shakespeare was born in Stratford-upon-Avon in 1564, and there are reasons to suppose that he came from a relatively prosperous family. He was probably educated at Stratford Grammar School and, at the age of eighteen, married Anne Hathaway, who was twenty-six. They had three children, a girl born shortly after their marriage, followed by twins in 1585 (the boy died in 1596). It seems likely that Shakespeare left for London shortly after a company of visiting players had visited Stratford in 1585, for by 1592 – according to the jealous testimony of one of his fellow-writers Robert Greene – he was certainly making his way both as actor and dramatist. The theatres were closed because of the plague in 1593; when they reopened Shakespeare worked with the Lord Chamberlain's men, later the King's men, and became a shareholder in each of the two theatres with which he was most closely associated, the Globe and the Blackfriars. He later purchased New Place, a considerable property in his home town of Stratford, to which he retired in 1611; there he entertained his great contemporary Ben Jonson (1572–1637) and the poet Michael Drayton (1563–1631). An astute businessman, Shakespeare lived comfortably in the town until his death in 1616.

This is a very brief outline of the life of our greatest writer, for little more can be said of him with certainty, though the plays – and poems – are living witness to the wisdom, humanity and many-faceted nature of the man. He was both popular and successful as a dramatist, perhaps less so as an actor. He probably began work as a dramatist in the late 1580s, by collaborating with other playwrights and adapting old plays, and by 1598 Francis Meres was paying tribute to his excellence in both comedy and tragedy. His first original play was probably *Love's Labour's Lost* (1590) and while the theatres were closed during the plague he wrote his narrative poems *Venus and Adonis* (1593) and *The Rape of Lucrece* (1594). The sonnets were almost certainly written in the 1590s though not published until 1609; the first 126 are addressed to a young man who was his friend and patron, while the rest are concerned with the 'dark lady'.

The dating of Shakespeare's plays has exercised scholars ever since the publication of the First Folio (1623), which listed them as comedies, histories and tragedies. It seems more important to look at them chronologically as far as possible, in order to trace Shakespeare's considerable development as a dramatist. The first period, say to the middle of the 1590s, included such plays as *Love's Labour's Lost*, *The Comedy of Errors*, *Richard III*, *The Taming of the Shrew*, *Romeo and Juliet* and *Richard II*. These early plays embrace the categories listed in the First Folio, so that Shakespeare the craftsman is evident in his capacity for variety of subject and treatment. The next phase includes *A Midsummer's Night's Dream*, *The Merchant of Venice*, *Henry IV Parts 1 and 2*, *Henry V* and *Much Ado About Nothing*, as well as *Julius Caesar*, *As You Like It* and *Twelfth Night*. These are followed, in the early years of the century, by his great tragic period: *Hamlet*, *Othello*, *King Lear* and *Macbeth*, with *Antony and Cleopatra* and *Coriolanus* belonging to 1607–09. The final phase embraces the romances (1610–13), *Cymbeline*, *The Tempest* and *The Winter's Tale* and the historical play *Henry VIII*.

Each of these revision aids will place the individual text under examination in the chronology of the remarkable dramatic output that spanned twenty years from the early 1590s to about 1613. The practical theatre for which Shakespeare wrote and acted derived from the inn courtyards in which performances had taken place, the few playhouses in his day being modelled on their structure. They were circular or hexagonal in shape, allowing the balconies and boxes around the walls full view of the stage. This large stage, which had no scenery, jutted out into the pit, the most extensive part of the theatre, where the poorer people – the 'groundlings' – stood. There was no roof (though the Blackfriars, used from 1608 onwards, was an indoor theatre) and thus bad weather meant no performance. Certain plays were acted at court, and these private performances normally marked some special occasion. Costumes, often rich ones, were used, and music was a common feature, with musicians on or under the stage; this sometimes had additional features, for example a trapdoor to facilitate the entry of a ghost. Women were barred by law from appearing on stage, and all female parts were played by boy actors; this undoubtedly explains the many instances in Shakespeare where a woman has to conceal her identity by disguising

herself as a man, e.g. Rosalind in *As You Like It*, Viola in *Twelfth Night*.

Shakespeare and his contemporaries often adapted their plays from sources in history and literature, extending an incident or a myth or creating a dramatic narrative from known facts. They were always aware of their own audiences, and frequently included topical references, sometimes of a satirical flavour, which would appeal to – and be understood by – the groundlings as well as their wealthier patrons who occupied the boxes. Shakespeare obviously learned much from his fellow dramatists and actors, being on good terms with many of them. Ben Jonson paid generous tribute to him in the lines prefaced to the First Folio of Shakespeare's plays:

Thou art a monument without a tomb,
And art alive still, while thy book doth live
And we have wits to read, and praise to give.

Among his contemporaries were Thomas Kyd (1558–94) and Christopher Marlowe (1564–93). Kyd wrote *The Spanish Tragedy*, the revenge motif here foreshadowing the much more sophisticated treatment evident in *Hamlet*, while Marlowe evolved the 'mighty line' of blank verse, a combination of natural speech and elevated poetry. The quality and variety of Shakespeare's blank verse owes something to the innovatory brilliance of Marlowe but carries the stamp of individuality, richness of association, technical virtuosity and, above all, the genius of imaginative power.

The texts of Shakespeare's plays are still rich sources for scholars, and the editors of these revision aids have used the Arden editions of Shakespeare, which are regarded as pre-eminent for their scholarly approach. They are strongly recommended for advanced students, but other editions, like The New Penguin Shakespeare, The New Swan, The Signet are all good annotated editions currently available. A reading list of selected reliable works on the play being studied is provided at the end of each commentary and students are advised to turn to these as their interest in the play deepens.

Literary terms used in these notes

Dramatic irony See section on p.92.

Metaphor A comparison which does not involve the use of 'like' or 'as'. For example, 'tongues in trees, books in the running brooks,/Sermons in stones' (Act II Scene 1)

Simile A comparison using 'like' or 'as' to introduce it: 'Which is as dry as the remainder biscuit/After a voyage' (Act II Scene 7)

Pun A word pronounced the same but capable of two meanings: 'I shall ne'er be ware of my own wit' (meaning both 'aware' of *and* 'be wary').

Word-play Where words are taken up and used in other associations by one or more speakers: 'Truly shepherd, in respect of itself, it is a good life; but in respect that it is a shepherd's life, it is naught. In respect that it is solitary, I like it very well; but in respect that it is private, it is a very vile life' (Act III Scene 2)

Personification Treating inanimate objects or abstract ideas as persons: 'doublet and hose ought to show itself courageous to petticoat' (Act II Scene 4).

Iambic pentameter The ten-syllabled line of unrhymed verse in *As You Like It*.

Octysyllabic lines i.e. having eight syllables in each line.

Couplets i.e. two lines having the same rhyme, generally called rhyming couplets.

Parody A deliberate use of the same form of verse, prose or phrasing which has been employed seriously for the purposes of mocking the sentiments of the original.

Analogy Similarity in a given number of features or details.

Satire The use of ridicule and irony to hold up to scorn certain topical issues.

Burlesque A ludicrous imitation or caricature of something with the intention of holding it up to ridicule.

The play
Plot, source, treatment and date

Plot

Orlando, the youngest son of his deceased father, Sir Rowland de Boys, is kept in servitude and ill-treated by his elder brother, Oliver. He rebels, having confided his anger to the old family retainer Adam, and resolves to try his fortune in a wrestling match at the court of Duke Frederick. The latter is the usurper who has driven his elder brother Duke Senior into exile in the forest of Arden. Oliver plots that the wrestler Charles will kill his brother, but Orlando wins the bout and promptly falls in love with Rosalind daughter of the banished Duke. She has seen the contest and fallen in love with him. Shortly after this, Rosalind is banished by Duke Frederick; Celia, her devoted friend and daughter of Frederick, suggests that they flee. Accompanied by the court clown Touchstone they depart, Rosalind disguised as a man (Ganymede) and Celia having assumed the name Aliena. Meanwhile Orlando is warned by Adam that Oliver plans to murder him and these two flee as well.

Eventually, and unknown to the other, each set of fugitives arrives in the forest of Arden where Duke Senior is living with those courtiers who have remained loyal to him. Among these is the 'melancholy' Jaques, who moralizes on life and nature and sometimes both. Orlando, searching for food for himself and Adam, reaches the Duke's court; Rosalind and Celia buy a sheep cote and Rosalind finds that Orlando is declaring his passion for her in verses and then hanging these on trees in the forest. When Orlando and Rosalind (Ganymede) finally meet, she suggests that she pretends to be Rosalind so that Orlando can woo her and thus ease his feelings. This mock-wooing certainly contributes humour to the action, which is further complicated by the arrival of Silvius and Phebe, a shepherd and shepherdess, the former in love with Phebe and the latter disdaining him. It is love at first sight when Phebe meets the disguised Rosalind despite having been reprimanded by her for her (Phebe's) treatment of Silvius.

Meanwile Oliver, despatched by the usurper Frederick, has come to the forest to arrest Orlando. The latter, however, rescues him from a lioness, who wounds Orlando. Oliver takes Orlando's bloody napkin to Rosalind, who faints, while Oliver reveals who he is and how he has repented his former treatment of his brother. Orlando and Celia fall in love at first sight. Rosalind contrives the four marriages which round off the play (for the clown Touchstone has picked up a country wench called Audrey) by shedding her disguise. Rosalind marries Orlando, Oliver marries Celia, Silvius marries Phebe, and Touchstone marries Audrey. Jaques de Boys arrives to bring the news that the usurping Duke has been converted to religion, and Duke Senior is thus restored to his former position and lands.

Source

Shakespeare based the plot of *As You Like It* on the pastoral novel *Rosalynde* by Thomas Lodge, which was published in 1590 and reprinted many times over the next few years. Lodge himself had taken part of his story from the *Tale of Gamelyn*, a 14th century poem, author unknown; he used from this the elder brother's ill-treatment of the younger brother, the loyal servant, the wrestling, the younger brother's flight. He added his own account of two rival kings, with the banishment of one by the other and the flight of the daughter of each to the forest of Arden where the banished king had taken refuge. Lodge's Rosalynde is also disguised as a boy, and the main love-story, the mock-wooing of Rosalind and the ill-treated younger brother, and the love-story of the shepherd and the shepherdess are also included. Lodge's ending, while happy, has all the love affairs resolved by marriage, but the banished king overthrows the usurping king in battle. Shakespeare undoubtedly took the whole story from Lodge, probably re-reading him shortly before he wrote *As You Like It*, or even while he was writing it. Most of Shakespeare's plays have one or more sources – sometimes these even being known to his audience – and he seems to have preferred to dramatize an existing story (with adaptations) rather than making up one himself.

Treatment of source

Shakespeare's alterations are basically of detail. Most of the names are changed, the rival kings become brother Dukes, while Ganymede/Rosalind becomes Aliena's brother not her page. In Lodge's story Aliena is rescued from robbers by the elder brother; Shakespeare omits this, and, striking a rare false note, omits too the battle and has the usurping Duke Frederick suddenly converted to the religious life instead. These slight changes in fact show Shakespeare's awareness of the tight structure of his own play, for example in the parallel stories of Sir Rowland's sons and that of the brother Dukes, with the stress on unnatural relationships in families. He enhances the nature of the romantic comedy by giving Rosalind a much more prominent role than Lodge had given her, while, and this shows a sureness of touch, the episode of Silvius and Phebe is less prominent in the play than it is in the novel. In Lodge's novel the king sends his own daughter into banishment for pleading for her cousin, but in *As You Like It* Celia decides on self-banishment, thus showing her independence, loyalty and love at the one stroke. Celia's character is enhanced by her offering to share Rosalind's fate.

Everything that is really great in *As You Like It* is Shakespeare's own, the scenes and actions having dramatic immediacy, the humour, wit, dialogue and poetry of the play deriving from the nature of his many-faceted imagination. There is little connection, for example, between Lodge's Rosalynde and Shakespeare's Rosalind in terms of spirit. And Shakespeare's originals Touchstone, Audrey, Jaques, Sir Oliver Martext, William and such minor but important structural figures as Le Beau and Amiens, are his coinage entirely. The story is merely a vehicle for his individualistic power.

Date of *As You Like It*

As You Like It appears in the Stationers' Register for August 1600, but there is no entry in the list given by Francis Meres in his *Palladis Tamia* in 1598. One theory suggests that the play was first written for private performance as part of the wedding celebrations of the Duke of Southampton in 1598, which would account for the concluding Hymen sequence. But an act of suppression against satirists belongs to 1599 (and Jaques is certainly a satirist), and the evidence for a concrete date swings back and forth. The Globe was opened in 1599, and Jaques's celebrated speech of 'All the world's a stage' might be in celebration of that event. Arguments for a much earlier date do not seem to hold up, despite the fact that Greene's adaptation of *Orlando Furioso*, performed in 1591, has some anticipations of Orlando's practice of hanging his verses to Rosalind on trees, as does Nashe's *Strange Newes*, published in 1592. There is one firm reference which puts the play in or after 1598. The playwright and poet Christopher Marlowe had been killed in a tavern brawl in 1593. Phebe actually quotes from Marlowe's *Hero and Leander*, which was not published until 1598. It seems probable, therefore, that the play was written in late 1598 – early 1599, and that it was performed sometime later in that year.

Scene summaries, critical commentaries, textual notes and revision questions

Act I Scene 1

Orlando is being kept in servitude by his brother Oliver, who at the same time has made full educational provision for the other brother Jaques (not to be confused with the melancholy Jaques who plays a much bigger role in the play). Orlando confides his dissatisfaction and suffering to the family's old retainer Adam. When Oliver appears the brothers first argue then come to blows, with Orlando threatening rebellion. When he and Adam are dismissed, Oliver sends for Charles the wrestler, who gives him the news that the old Duke has been banished by his younger brother. The old Duke is now in exile, his lands having been confiscated by his younger brother. We learn that Rosalind, the old Duke's daughter, still remains in the court with Celia, the usurping Duke's daughter, and that the two girls are inseparable friends. Charles further reveals that he is to wrestle on the following day, and that he has heard that Orlando will try to take him on. Oliver and Charles plan Orlando's death, and Oliver, at the end of the scene, ponders on his brother's popularity.

Commentary

The function of this scene is to establish some of the themes of the play: brother is set against brother, Orlando/Oliver, Duke Frederick/Duke Senior. The scene is fittingly in prose, since the theme is corruption and usurpation, and does not merit the use of blank verse. There is every indication of Orlando's spirit and strength, and a passing reference to the close relationship between Rosalind and Celia, a relationship which never gives way under pressure. The skill of the dramatist is immediately evident, since this opening is subtly contrived to make us think more of tragedy than comedy. Also evident is the nature/nurture contrast which is to run throughout the play: Orlando being noble by nature and Oliver evil perhaps by nature and by nurture, the nurture of the court which invites corruption. This latter is evidenced when Charles speaks of the old Duke's exile, and the theme of loyalty – symbolized by Adam to Orlando, Celia to Rosalind – is stressed when we learn that some of the old Duke's lords have joined him in exile in the Forest of Arden. The degree of Oliver's corruption, and the nature of his jealousy, is shown in his instructions to Charles, yet ironically his own appraisal of Orlando's character is accurate. We note too Oliver's cunning in drawing Charles out before he reveals what he really feels about Orlando. With the wrestling imminent, the scene ends on a note of expectation and dramatic tension.

poor a thousand A mere thousand.
on his blessing i.e. in order to honour (his father's wishes).
breed me well Educate me properly.
school This is vague, but it perhaps means what we would call advanced or university education.
goldenly Glowingly.
profit Advance, achievement.
stays me Keeps me.
unkept i.e. not properly provided for.
stalling Confining in a stall.
fair with their feeding i.e. fed heathily.
taught their manage Properly trained in their paces.
bound Indebted.
countenance Restrictive treatment, and perhaps disapproving looks.
hinds Farm workers.
as much as in him lies As far as he can.
mines my gentility i.e. undermines my noble birth.
Go apart Stand to one side.
shake me up Treat me badly (either verbally or physically).
make A pun on (a) do and (b) construct, work at in Orlando's reply.
Marry This is a mild oath, reduced from 'By the Virgin Mary', here equivalent to 'Indeed'.
be naught awhile Be quiet a minute.
husks The chaff of wheat and dry outer seed cases.
prodigal portion A reference to the parable of the Prodigal Son (Luke 15, 11–32). The younger brother took his portion of their inheritance and, having wasted it, had to work with little to eat in a stranger's fields.
orchard Garden.
the gentle condition of blood By virtue of our being closely related.
know me Accept me in the same way.
The courtesy of nations The custom of civilized countries.
albeit Although.
your coming . . . reverence Your being older than me entitles you to more respect.

young Inexperienced. The opposite of an 'old hand', here used in contrast to 'elder'.

villain Scoundrel (or of low birth).

railed on Abused.

accord i.e. at peace with one another.

exercises i.e. education, training.

allottery Rightful share.

testament Will.

will A pun on (a) legacy and (b) wish.

becomes Is fitting for.

Is it even so? Is that how it is?

grow upon Increase so as to become more troublesome (like weeds).

physic your rankness Remedy your offensiveness (continuing the image of growth of weeds – cut down your vegetation).

no . . . neither The double negative is correct grammatically and used here for emphasis.

importunes Presses for.

'Twill be a good way The implication is 'This is a good opportunity'.

old Duke . . . new Duke i.e. Duke Senior and Duke Frederick respectively.

good leave to wander i.e. freedom to go (since he now has their estates).

that she would have followed . . . i.e. that she (Celia) would have followed Rosalind into exile, an ironic foreshadowing of what actually happens.

Forest of Arden The Ardennes forest in north-east France, but there is also an area of this name in Warwickshire near Stratford, where Shakespeare was born.

Robin Hood The legendary outlaw and hero, the comparison with Duke Senior investing the latter with a kind of heroic stature.

fleet Pass.

golden world Age of peace and plenty, according to the classical authors.

disposition Inclination.

fall i.e. a wrestling match.

credit Reputation.

foil Overcome.

come in i.e. takes me on, wrestles with me.

withal With this.

brook Bear, put up with.

disgrace Loss of reputation.

search i.e. seeking it himself, the implication being that he (Orlando) will be responsible for his own defeat.

requite Reward.

purpose herein Intention here.

underhand means Indirect methods.

envious emulator Vicious, jealous copier (of others).

good parts Personal qualities.

contriver Plotter.

natural brother Note the irony of his 'unnatural' in view of his treatment of Orlando.

discretion Judgement.

had as leif Should be just as happy if.

look to't Watch out.

mightily grace himself i.e. greatly increase his reputation (at your expense).

practise . . . poison Plot . . . evil methods.

anatomize Reveal in great detail.

payment i.e. what he deserves.

go alone Walk unaided.

gamester Sporting man.

never schooled and yet learned i.e. never had the benefit of education yet he has acquired knowledge.

noble device Gentlemanly behaviour and ideas.

of all sorts By everyone.

in the heart of the world Loved by everyone.

misprised Unappreciated, undervalued.

shall not be so long Will not continue this way.

clear all Resolve everything.

kindle the boy thither Stir him (Orlando) to go and wrestle (with Charles).

Act I Scene 2

The second scene opens with Celia trying to cheer up Rosalind, who is brooding about her banished father. Celia says that she will repay Rosalind in the future for what her (Rosalind's) father has lost, and Rosalind replies by suggesting that they decide how to pass the time. They are interrupted by the clown Touchstone, who has come to summon Celia to her father. This exchange is further interrupted by Le Beau, who brings news of the wrestling and the triumph of Charles over three young men. The Duke Frederick and his attendants enter prior to the wrestling between Charles and Orlando. Rosalind tries to dissuade Orlando from wrestling for fear he might be injured. However, she need not worry as he defeats Charles and then reveals his true identity to Duke Frederick. Rosalind gives Orlando a chain to wear for her sake: she and Orlando have fallen in love at first sight. Le Beau returns to urge Orlando to leave and reveals to him that Rosalind is the banished Duke's daughter.

Commentary

Celia's spirit, and her genuine love for Rosalind, is demonstrated by her generosity. Again prose is used to convey the sadness of Rosalind's state. The discussion between the two on love, fortune and nature shows the witty and intelligent nature of each. Touchstone reveals his capacity for word-play, which is one of the main features of *As You Like It*, and he also demonstrates that he can be very wordy. Le Beau symbolizes the gossipy and sycophantic courtier, but the dramatic tension is raised by his account of the wrestling, since we are already in anticipation of Charles's bout with Orlando. Before that, Rosalind and Celia have good, witty sport at the expense of Le Beau, but Rosalind shows her own vulnerability, how easily she is moved to sympathy, when she learns of the fate of the old man's three sons. She is further moved, as is Celia, when they reason with Orlando to abandon his attempt. His quick success, the Duke's reaction to his identity, his obvious love for Rosalind (and hers for him — 'My pride fell with my fortunes') indicate the pace of this scene, which is sad, then witty, then full of action. Yet the tone is sombre, with Orlando and Rosalind both using metaphors from wrestling, the first to convey her falling in love, the second to explain his tongue-tied response to Rosalind. Le Beau's role – to announce the wrestling and to urge Orlando to leave – is functional. Curiously he describes Celia as the 'taller' of the two, though later we know that Rosalind, who assumes male disguise, is certainly taller than Celia. With Orlando victorious and elevated to his rightful nobility, blank verse is used to underline this and also to signal the romantic nature of the developing action.

coz Cousin.
am mistress of Possess.
learn Teach.
weight Feeling, concern.
so As long as.
take Accept.
so wouldst thou You would have done the same.
righteously tempered Completely blended.
condition of my estate My circumstances.
perforce By force.
render Hand back to (with legal implications).

monster i.e. behave unnaturally, wickedly, inhumanly.

henceforth From this time forward.

devise sports Plan amusements.

prithee Please.

in good earnest Completely.

a pure blush (a) slight embarrassment (b) maidenly appearance.

come off Disengage.

mock . . . wheel Ridicule her so that she leaves, implying that the blind goddess turning the Wheel of Fate is no better than a common housewife at her spinning wheel.

misplaced Put into the wrong hands (Rosalind is thinking of her own 'fate').

bountiful blind woman i.e. the blind goddess of fortune with her gifts to bestow.

most mistake i.e. is in greatest error.

honest Virtuous, chaste.

ill-favouredly Of unpleasing appearance, ugly.

office Area of authority.

gifts of the world Material things.

lineaments of Nature i.e. personal qualities.

sent in this fool i.e. sent Touchstone here to stop our discussion.

hard Strong.

natural Born fool, dim-wit.

Peradventure Maybe.

to reason of To discuss, debate.

goddesses i.e. of Nature or Fortune.

whetstone Sharpening stone (for our wit – and note the half-pun with 'Touchstone').

Wit Here used playfully to address Touchstone.

Wander (a) walking about (b) a play on the rambling wits of the idiot, 'wandering' in his mind.

messenger (a) bearer of messages (b) arresting officer. Celia is being witty about Touchstone's function here.

naught No good.

stand to it Swear on oath.

forsworn Guilty of perjury, having broken his oath.

great heap Vast amount (Rosalind is being very sarcastic).

forth Forward, into view.

chins . . . beards This is a cunning and unobtrusive anticipation of the disguise adopted by Celia and Rosalind later, though they don't have beards!

knave Rascal.

My father's love . . . i.e. the fact that my father loves him is enough to demonstrate that he is honourable.

whipped for taxation Punished for criticizing.

The more pity . . . It's a shame that we fools cannot use our wisdom to comment on the foolishness of so-called wise men.

By my troth Upon my faith, truly.

since the little wit . . . show This probably refers to the recent public burning of satirical pamphlets. This foolish act of supposedly wise men made 'a great show', but Celia's comment also applies to the arrival of a 'showy' courtier, Le Beau.

news Gossip.

pigeons feed their young i.e. by regurgitating the food that the adult birds have partially digested and which is crammed roughly into the gaping beaks of their young.

marketable Valuable, as gossips with plenty of news, or well-fed poultry.

colour Kind.

Destinies The three Fates (or Parcae) of Roman mythology who controlled the lives of men.

laid on with a trowel i.e. like mortar, applied without refinement, bluntly spoken.

keep . . . rank (a) don't retain my place (as a jester) (b) lose my offensive smell – the latter phrase is immediately taken up by Rosalind.

amaze Confuse.

lost the sight of i.e. you have missed it (the wrestling).

match . . . tale i.e. that beginning is certainly a common one.

proper Worthy.

with bills . . . presents' Rosalind's interruption picks up the word 'presents', imagining the three sons with 'bills' or billhooks on their shoulders. Then they become labelled with legal bills. The private joke is lost on Le Beau.

served Treated, dealt with.

dole Sorrowing, grieving.

broken music (a) the sound of wailing (b) bones breaking.

sides i.e. where the ribs are.

sure Certainly.

his own peril The risk is entirely his.

forwardness Boldness.

successfully Confident of success.

liege Lord.

odds Balance of advantage (with Charles).

fain Gladly.

move him Change his mind.

by Present.

the Princess This is typical of Le Beau's exaggerated language and servility.

attend Wait upon.

saw . . . eyes i.e. could see yourself as others see you.

knew yourself with your judgement i.e. estimate your chances as others estimate them.

counsel you to a more equal enterprise i.e. advise you to undertake a more equal match.

give over Abandon.

misprized See note p.19.

suit Petition, request.

punish me not with your hard thoughts wherein . . . guilty Do not think badly of me although I know in this respect I deserve it.

foiled Thrown.

never gracious Not smiled on by Fortune.

eke out Add to, make last longer.

deceived in you Mistaken in my judgement of your strength.

working Task (Orlando refers to his 'humble' determination to win).

You shall try but one fall i.e. the contest ends when one of you is thrown down.

warrant Guarantee.

You mean to mock me after (Even if) you expect to laugh at me after (you have won), you shouldn't laugh before, i.e. don't laugh too soon.

come your ways i.e. let's get on with it.

Hercules . . . speed May the god of physical strength be the bringer of success to you.

well breathed Even winded.

my liege Orlando acknowledges that he owes allegiance to the Duke.

still Always.

Were I my father Celia is amazed at her father's reaction and behaviour.

that calling (a) being called that (b) that station in life.

given him tears unto entreaties Added tears to my pleas to him not to fight (i.e. tried even harder).

encourage Commend, praise.

envious Malicious.

Sticks Stabs.

But justly i.e. just as well.

one out of suits with fortune i.e. not wearing the mark of favour, not being fortunate (at the moment).

could Would.

parts i.e. nature.

quintain Tilting target (in jousting), a dummy.

He . . . back Rosalind is reduced to this invention by Orlando's inability to speak. She gives him another chance, something that pride would have prevented her from doing formerly.

overthrown . . . enemies Rosalind is using the wrestling metaphor to show that her own heart has been 'overthrown' by Orlando. She loves him at first sight.

Have with you This is a good-natured rebuff, telling Celia that she understands her concern.

urg'd conference Encouraged conversation.

Or . . . or Either . . . or.

something weaker i.e. Rosalind (the weaker sex).

counsel Advise.

Albeit Although.
condition Mood.
misconsters Misconstrues, misinterprets.
humorous Given to moodiness.
More suits you . . . speak of It would be more fitting for you to imagine than for me to say.
taller A confusing detail, since in the next scene Rosalind suggests that she herself is the taller.
Hath ta'en displeasure Has conceived a hatred.
argument Basis.
smother Smouldering fire, suffocating smoke.
from tyrant Duke i.e. escaping from one peril only to fall into a greater one (and note that the scene is virtually rounded off with a rhyming couplet, a favourite Shakespearian device).

Act I Scene 3

Rosalind, very much in love with Orlando, is teased by Celia because of her silence. Despite this, she manages some repartee, and urges Celia to love Orlando for her sake. Duke Frederick enters dramatically and banishes Rosalind from the court. Threatened with death within ten days if she does not go, Rosalind reasons with the Duke to no avail. Celia joins her voice to Rosalind's and asserts her love for the latter, but the Duke considers that Celia has been duped by Rosalind's cunning. Celia asserts that 'she cannot live out of her company' and opts to accompany Rosalind into exile. They decide to flee to the Forest of Arden to seek out Rosalind's father. Rosalind is to be disguised as a man, Jove's page Ganymede, Celia will take the name Aliena, and Touchstone will join with them.

Commentary

Again rapid dramatic development is the keynote of this scene. Rosalind's love for Orlando is poignantly revealed, but she never loses her capacity for punning and verbal play, even in adversity. Celia is assuredly her equal in terms of wit. Duke Frederick is shown as obdurate, unscrupulous and cruel, Celia as loyal and imaginative, for she is the active planner of their flight. Again we are aware of the motives of power and jealousy, with some duplication of situation. The Duke is determined to maintain his power, as was Oliver, and will rid himself of any threat, here Rosalind, who is popular with the people (like Orlando). There is a certain irony in the use of blank verse once the Duke appears, for we must remember that his is a usurped nobility. Celia's wit is equal to the crisis ('Wilt thou change fathers? I will give thee mine'), while her assertion of loyalty to and love for Rosalind gives the scene a particularly moving quality. Rosalind is almost overcome by Celia's practicality, but rallies to invent her own disguise with something approaching satirical verve. The decision to take Touchstone covers the girls' inherent fear of being attacked and robbed (or raped), and Celia again shows her zest for the flight and her down-to-earth nature by making sure that they take 'our jewels and our wealth together'.

Cupid The Roman God of Love. Celia suspects the reason for Rosalind's silence.

to throw at a dog i.e. either a bone or a stone to make it go away.

laid up Sick (as Rosalind is already 'sick' with love).

mad without any i.e. because she has lost her reason.

my child's father i.e. the man whose child I would bear.

working-day Everyday.

burs As opposed to 'briars', since they only catch lightly on the clothing and are thrown in fun.

trodden paths i.e. (if we) behave unconventionally.

Hem A pun on (a) clear the throat and (b) stitch (referring back to petticoats).

cry hem Rosalind is punning on 'him' (Orlando) and 'hem', the clearing of the throat which attracts attention.

wrestle . . . affections Try to control your emotions (with a continuation of the wrestling metaphor).

take the part of Are on the side of.

a good wish upon you Good luck to you.

cry in time In due course (you will cry out in labour, conceive).

a fall Celia is still playing on the wrestling metaphor.

turning . . . service Joking apart.

By this kind of chase Following this kind of reasoning.

Why should I not? This is ambiguous. She may be saying 'Why shouldn't I hate him?' or perhaps 'Why shouldn't I do that?' i.e. hate him not.

for that i.e. what he deserves.

dispatch you with your safest haste i.e. the sooner you go, the safer you will be.

If . . . intelligence If I am in touch with my own understanding.

frantic Insane.

thought unborn i.e. subconsciously.

purgation Clearing (themselves) from blame.

grace i.e. goodness.

suffice thee Be good enough for you.

the likelihood depends The possibility arises.

Dear sovereign Celia addresses her father officially, not as a loving daughter would.

rang'd along Been in the same situation.

that time Then.

still Always.

like Juno's swans i.e. harnessed together. Swans are normally associated with Venus rather than Juno, who was the wife of Jupiter, ruler of the Gods in Roman mythology.

coupled Together.

subtle Cunning.

robs thee of thy name i.e. gets the praise and is shown the honour that you should get.

virtuous Noble in quality.

doom Sentence.

provide Prepare.

in the greatness of my word i.e. since I have the power to command.

charge Command.

sunder'd Separated.

devise Plan.

change i.e. of circumstances.

heaven . . . pale i.e. the implication is that the skies grow pale in sympathy with their sufferings.

what thou canst Whatever you want.

Beauty provoketh thieves Rosalind is thinking of their vulnerability to rape.

mean Humble.

umber Brown pigment.

The like do you You do the same.

common tall i.e. above the average height.

suit me Dress myself.

all points In all respects.

gallant Brave-looking, fashionable.

curtle-axe Cutlass, short sword.

hidden Secret.

a swashing and a martial outside A swaggering and a warlike appearance.

outface it Bluff it out.

semblances Outward appearances (which may hide the truth).

Jove's own page . . . Ganymede The latter was a mortal chosen for his beauty who became the cup-bearer of Jove (Jupiter).

Aliena From the Latin which means 'the one who is estranged'.

Revision questions on Act I

1 Write an essay on the speed of the dramatic action in this act.
2 Demonstrate Shakespeare's use of contrast and parallel in this act.
3 It has been said that Rosalind is overshadowed by Celia at the beginning of the play. Do you agree? Refer to the text in support of your views.
4 What do we learn in this act of the characters of (a) Celia (b) Duke Frederick (c) Orlando (d) Oliver?
5 Write an essay on Shakespeare's use of verse and prose in this act.
6 Indicate the part played by the wrestling, showing its influence on Rosalind and Orlando.

Act II Scene 1

This contrasts with the first act as a whole, for we move to the other 'court', that of the exiles in the Forest of Arden. The banished Duke's first speech describes the freedom of nature, and he obliquely compares it to the court. He decides to hunt, and the first lord tells him of Jaques's moralizing on the killing of the deer. In a sense, Jaques feels that they, the usurped courtiers, are usurping the haunts of nature. The Duke is anxious to see him in this kind of mood.

Commentary

This short scene shows the movement of the plot, since from now on with the exception of two brief scenes and Orlando's meeting with Adam before Oliver's house, the action of the play is concentrated in the forest. Contrast is of the essence both in Duke Senior's speech and in the reportage of Jaques's moralizing. 'Painted pomp', 'the envious court' and 'this is no flattery' show how 'sweet are the uses of adversity', and despite the idealization, the language is finely appropriate, with reference to the seasons and at the same time an imagery to describe the 'language' of nature. There is even compassion in the Duke's acknowledgement that it is a shame to kill the deer who are 'native burghers of this desert city', and this and other images maintain the nature/court contrast which is at the heart of the play. The account of the 'melancholy Jaques' (a foretaste of his determined affectation) carries with it an ironic humour, for if the death of the stag is overdone in terms of moralizing, it is also romantically observed, with Jaques's 'thousand similes' sending up the fact that death is a matter for exaggerated images. Jaques's analogies in which he 'pierceth through/The body of country, city, court/Yea, and of this our life' stress the contrasts and similiarities already mentioned. The economy is marked, the language elevated and satirical, with blank verse employed to stress the essentially elevated nature of the banished Duke.

old custom Habit. They are getting used to the life.
penalty of Adam Loss of the state of innocence, and therefore subject to suffering.
icy fang Biting cold (and note the harsh animal image).
counsellors Advisers (the Duke is emphasizing the court/nature contrast so typical of this play).
feelingly Through the sensations of my body, strongly.
Sweet are the uses of adversity It is good to be able to profit from misfortune.
toad . . . jewel There was a popular superstition that the toad had a precious stone in its head which could be used as an antidote to poison. The toad itself was thought to be poisonous to the touch.
exempt from public haunt Free from crowds.
tongues Conversation, language (of nature).
books Stories (of natural life – growth etc).
Sermons The Duke's idealization of nature continues, this last word giving it a religious, spiritual value.
translate (a) explain (b) interpret nature in this way.
stubbornness Toughness.
style (a) way of life (b) literary composition.
dappled fools Roe-deer have dappled markings, and 'fools' here is a term of endearment.
burghers Citizens (a continuation of the city/nature analogy).
desert Uncultivated.
fork'd heads i.e. arrows, but perhaps also thinking of horns.
gor'd Pierced, wounded.
kind Manner.
along Stretched out.
antique Ancient.
brawls Chatters noisily.
sequester'd Separated, i.e. cut off from the herd.
ta'en a hurt Been wounded.
languish Grow weaker and more distressed.
discharge Release.

leathern coat Hide.
Cours'd Followed, chased.
Much marked of Closely watched by.
extremest verge Very edge.
moralize this spectacle Draw morals or lessons from this sight.
similes Comparisons (and note the mocking tone at Jaques's
  affectations).
worldlings People of the world (spoken rather sneeringly).
sum of more Addition.
velvet friend i.e. the coat of the deer and the velvet coat worn by a
  courtier.
misery . . . flux of company i.e. grief, sadness stops the flow of life.
Anon Later.
Full of the pasture Well-fed.
greasy i.e. soiled with the signs of good living.
just the fashion i.e. that's the way of life.
Wherefore Why.
bankrupt One without anything left (still continuing the city/nature
  analogy).
invectively With violent words.
pierceth through i.e. as with a verbal rapier, he attacked in turn the
  city, the country, the court, and their ways of life.
kill them up Destroy them.
assign'd Appointed (by God).
cope Come up against.
matter i.e. subject matter, things to discuss.
straight Immediately.

Act II Scene 2

This short scene shows Duke Frederick learning of the flight of
Celia and Rosalind. Touchstone has also gone, and it is sus-
pected that Orlando has accompanied them. Believing this,
Duke Frederick demands that Oliver be sent for if Orlando
cannot be found.

Commentary

This is a functional scene, showing the effects of the flight of
Celia and Rosalind, and also preparing for the banishment of
Oliver in Act III. The account of the eavesdropping is a further
comment on the practices and insecurity of the court. The Duke
needs to be told in order to maintain his power whilst the
gentlewoman needs to report what she heard in order to be sure

of keeping her position. The comment, even in this short scene, is on the morality of such behaviour.

villains (a) serfs (b) scoundrels.
untreasur'd i.e. empty.
roynish Coarse, common.
was wont Used.
sinewy Muscular and strong.
his brother i.e. Oliver.
inquisition quail Questioning fail.

Act II Scene 3

Adam warns Orlando that Oliver, having heard of his triumph, plans to burn down the house with him inside it that night. At first Orlando says that he will stay and confront Oliver, but Adam reveals that he has saved some money over the long years that he worked for Orlando's father. Orlando, moved, agrees to go away with him to 'some settled low content'.

Commentary

The nobility of Adam's emotions, despite his lowly status, means that the whole scene is written in blank verse. The theme is loyalty, with the emphasis on the further corruption of Oliver, the dramatic possibility of the fire, the self-sacrificing (and somewhat wordy) nature of Adam, and the unaffected moralizing of both Adam and Orlando. The latter asserts his pride and independence, but is forced to give in to the goodness of Adam. The latter ascribes his health to abstemiousness in youth, so that the moral theme – here somewhat unconvincing – is still being given a considered stress. There is a nostalgic emphasis too on the theme that 'things are not as they once were', and the scene is rounded off with a succession of rather cloying rhyming couplets. Seen in the context of goodness versus evil, one of the major elements of the play, this is structurally important, but it is somewhat stereotypical. Just as the Duke represents evil, so Adam represents loyalty, service, goodness. But we note the loyalty perhaps most of all – a direct parallel with Celia's loyalty to Rosalind.

memory Reminder (by his appearance).
make you Are you doing.
virtuous Noble.
fond Foolish enough.
bonny prizer Sturdy prize-fighter.
humorous i.e. subject to bad moods.
too swiftly home i.e. suddenly.
Their graces serve them i.e. their achievements tell against them.
No more do yours Your graces will tell against you.
Your virtues . . . to you What you have done will act to your detriment.
comely Pleasing, proper.
within Under.
use to lie i.e. where you usually stay.
cut you off i.e. kill you.
practices Plots.
butchery Slaughterhouse.
boist'rous Violent.
enforce Make for myself.
do how I can Whatever may happen to me.
subject me Give myself up.
diverted blood i.e. unnatural behaviour.
thrifty hire i.e. carefully saved from my wages.
foster-nurse i.e. security.
service . . . lame i.e. when I am too old to work.
unregarded (a) not thought to be of value (b) not taken care of.
He . . . ravens . . . sparrow i.e. God (see Luke, 12, 6 and 24).
lusty Healthy.
apply Take.
rebellious i.e. revolting, causing me to indulge myself sinfully.
unbashful forehead Immodest thoughts.
woo Invite.
debility Feebleness.
The constant service of the antique world The faithful duties of the
  past.
sweat for duty, not for meed i.e. when all was done by hard work and
  not just for reward.
fashion of these times Present practices.
choke i.e. as weeds do (nature and man contrasted again).
thou prun'st a rotten tree i.e. your efforts cannot be rewarded.
lieu Place.
pains and husbandry Efforts and economy.
come thy ways Come along.
ere Before.
youthful wages i.e. earned in the days of your youth.
light Come across.
settled low content Steady, modest, satisfactory condition.
too late a week i.e. far too late.

recompense Reward. Note the rhyming couplets which round off the
scene.

Act II Scene 4

Rosalind as Ganymede and Celia as Aliena (we retain their real
names for the purposes of this commentary) arrive in the Forest
of Arden with Touchstone. They are weary, but continue to
employ their verbal wit on and with Touchstone. They meet
Corin and Silvius, the latter a young rustic in love with a disdainful shepherdess Phebe. Rosalind and Celia buy a cottage pasture
and flock from the old man Corin, Celia being almost faint from
want of food. No mention is made of the exiled Duke.

Commentary

Silvius's avowal of love for Phebe prepares the audience for the
later Phebe episode, and further complicates the love-tangle of
the final scenes of the play. Rosalind's personality now begins to
assert itself – she is away from the court, and there is a fine irony
in the way she is already enjoying her role as a man. The
entrance of Silvius provides a romantic elevation into blank
verse, since this is a Shakespearian satire on romantic love and
the pastoral convention. There is a noteworthy parallelism here
too, since the extremes of love felt by Sylvius are also felt by
Rosalind, who identifies herself with Silvius's expressions, and
also by Orlando, who is shortly to decorate the trees in the forest
with effusions to Rosalind. Touchstone in reminiscence provides
his own comic equivalent – and a coarse one it is too – to these
romantic sighings. Thus a running humour accompanies the
romance, for Touchstone's earthy examples provide a nice
balance at the other extreme, and in fact prepare us for the
scenes involving Audrey. Notice the focus on love, the main
theme of the play.

Jupiter See note on Ganymede p.26. An appropriate oath for
Ganymede.
the weaker vessel i.e. Celia, the woman.
doublet and hose i.e. the man's jacket and breeches she is wearing.
courageous to petticoat i.e. the man (which Rosalind is affecting to be)
ought to protect the woman.
cannot go no further Here the double negative is used for emphasis.

cross (a) burden (b) coin with a cross, i.e. money.
wast Were.
many actions most ridiculous Much foolish behaviour.
fantasy Delusion.
run into Commit.
broke from company i.e. forsaken society.
searching . . . wound Probing your weakness.
hard adventure Misfortune.
him i.e. the stone, but standing in place of a rival lover.
batler Wooden implement used to beat clothes in the wash.
dugs Udders.
chopt Chapped, cracked.
peascod Peapod.
cods Pods.
mortal (a) destined to die (b) extreme. Touchstone is underlining the
  fact that lovers commit lovers to do foolish things.
art ware i.e. are aware.
be ware Punning on 'be aware' and 'be warned'.
break my shins Trip over.
much upon my fashion Just how I feel.
stale i.e. rather tiresome.
yond That.
clown Peasant and fool (ironic that Touchstone should use such a
  term, being the 'fool' himself).
Else are they very wretched i.e. they would have to be very wretched
  indeed not to be better than me.
desert Lonely.
entertainment Food and somewhere to stay.
travel much oppress'd i.e. exhausted by her journey.
relieve her Help her.
churlish disposition Mean nature.
little recks Takes hardly any trouble.
cote Cottage.
bounds of feed Pasturelands.
in my voice As far as I am able to make you.
swain Countryman (a term also used of country lovers, particularly in
  pastoral verse).
but erewhile A short time ago.
stand with honesty i.e. is not a dishonest thing for you to do.
to pay for it of us i.e. we shall provide the money for you to buy it.
mend Raise.
report Investigation.
feeder i.e. workman, looking after animals.
right suddenly Forthwith, at once.

Act II Scene 5

This has Amiens singing in praise of nature, a theme which Jaques finds attractive, though he comments rather cynically throughout. Meanwhile the preparation of the Duke's banquet is continuing, and Amiens and Jaques engage in banter, with Jaques capping Amiens's song with a small cynical gem of his own.

Commentary

This scene sustains the happy forest atmosphere through the use of Amiens's song, which simply praises nature and the open air life. Jaques's comments show the sharpness of his tongue and his ability to draw from past experience material for acidic comment. Jaques is not only melancholy, he is also indolent, trying to avoid the Duke rather than be forced into reasoning. His own song is a deliberate parody of the ideals in Amiens's song, and we note that he doesn't want his sleep disturbed, a further indication of his nature. He contributes greatly to the word-play and range of association in this scene. Again we note the pattern of contrast with the previous scene – the sufferings of Rosalind and Celia – and the one which follows, the sufferings of Adam. This scene reflects, if you like, the good life; elsewhere in the forest others are tasting a far from sweet adversity.

greenwood The natural forest; 'going to the greenwood' meant becoming an outlaw.
turn Change.
I thank it I'm grateful for it.
ragged Rough.
stanzo Verse.
they owe me nothing i.e. I only remember the names of people who owe me money.
compliment Courtly behaviour.
th' encounter . . . apes A ritual involving much grinning and behaviour to establish supremacy.
beggarly i.e. as a beggar would.
cover the while Set the table in the meantime.
disputable Argumentative.
matters Subjects.
note Song.
in despite of my invention i.e. although my imagination is none too good.

turn ass Becomes foolish.
Ducdame Probably 'Come with me', of Welsh derivation.
Gross As great.
And if Provided that.
a Greek invocation i.e. an unintelligible calling up of spirits – compare
  this with the modern expression 'It's all Greek to me'.
circle Witches dance in a circle, but the shape has always been
  associated with magic.
rail against Curse.
the first-born of Egypt Eldest sons, referring to 'the loving lords' who
  lost their estates by following the Duke into exile. In the Bible, the
  first-born of Egypt lost their lives in the last of the plagues. This led to
  the release of the Israelites from captivity. See Exodus 12 and 29.
  Jaques's 'threatened curse' would be designed to obtain his release
  from the life in the forest which he claims to find disagreeable.

Act II Scene 6

Orlando and Adam have now arrived in the forest. Adam is near
collapse from want of food.

Commentary

This short scene is functional, its object being to stress the
contrast mentioned above and, most importantly, to bring the
principal characters teasingly in reach of each other. This again
makes for dramatic tension.

measure out i.e. stretch full out, as though measuring the area
  required for a grave.
uncouth Unfamiliar, desolate.
savage i.e. like a wild animal.
conceit Imagination.
powers Physical abilities.
presently Immediately.
leave Permission.
a mocker of my labour i.e. you undermine my efforts.
Well said! That's better!
bleak Exposed.

Act II Scene 7

The Duke's banquet, with Jaques entering to tell of his encounter with Touchstone. He is mightily pleased with him, for

Touchstone has been moralizing on fortune and time. Jaques comes to the satisfactory conclusion (for him) that 'Motley's the only wear.' Jaques indulges the fancy that he would like to be a fool himself. He would then have the liberty and license to express his views on life, even to the point that he would 'Cleanse the foul body of th' infected world.' The Duke reminds him that he (Jaques) has indulged in all the sensual pleasures in his youth Jaques counters by excusing himself for being satirical and argues that the meaning of his satire, depends on interpretation: what applies to one man may or may not apply to another. At this juncture Orlando appears with his sword in readiness, and the Duke invites him to join their meal; Orlando, moved by his kindness, relinquishes his threats, says that he will go to get Adam, and Jaques makes the most of the occasion with his 'All the world's a stage' speech. Orlando returns with Adam, Amiens sings an appropriate song, and the Duke learns that Orlando is Sir Rowland's son.

Commentary

The variety in this scene is remarkable, with Jaques turning his mind to the contemplation of Touchstone (there are cynical points of contact between them), his account being humorous, witty, even graphic. By a subtle ironic juxtaposition, his report of Touchstone's noting the passage of time counterbalances his own great 'All the world's a stage' which is to come, for 'thereby hangs a tale'. We see into the character of Jaques, whose appreciation of Touchstone is itself a satirical comment on court life and values, and his assertion of freedom to say what he wishes, an effective contrast both with the over-idealization on the one hand and the corruption on the other. The Duke's tone is moral, recalling Jaques's libertine past, but Jaques's reply, while it puts a low premium on human nature (because people are basically sinful and alike) is a brilliant piece of rhetorical self-justification. The drama and pathos of Orlando's entrance is very effective after Jaques's long-winded speech; his reponse to the kindness of the Duke is moving, and is given a certain spiritual and humanitarian quality by the effective repetition of 'If ever . . .'. In fact the references to bells and churches give their exchange a practical Christian element obviously intended to balance the evil in the play. Even the imagery 'like a doe, I go to find my fawn' reverses the hunting analogies of the earlier scenes, and anticipates the themes of repentance and reconciliation by its human emphasis. The Duke prepares the way for Jaques's fine extended simile comparing the world to the theatre, a rhetorical masterpiece, cynical, but rich in vivid word pictures of the life of man from the cradle to the grave. It is a set-piece, much anthologized, but we should study it not merely for its wisdom and realism, but also for its sublime irony, the irony which uses the author's own medium – the play – as the basis for comparison. Plays, like life, have their phases from beginning to end of action, from birth to death, and in Jaques's words Shakespeare is contemplating ironically and realistically his own craft. There is a further comment; his words, and particularly speeches like this, have survived life and death, living on through the generations that come and go. Life is ephemeral; the words of genius, immortal. After this, a further contrast is achieved through the balancing use of song, for the cynicism of Jaques is underlined by references like 'man's ingratitude', 'Most friendship is feigning' 'most loving mere folly' and 'friend remember'd not'. This in its turn is put into perspective by the genuine kindness of the Duke to old Adam; man in adversity helps man against the background of nature, a telling contrast with the thrusting ambition and corruption of court life. Gradually the characters are being brought together. Orlando's revelation that he is Sir Rowland's son shows the emergence of good over evil, another constant theme in the play.

compact of jars Made up of disharmonies and disagreements.
in the spheres The movement of the spheres around the earth was thought to produce perfect musical harmony.
motley i.e. the distinctive dress of the fool.
a miserable world i.e. what a world we live in.
good set terms Logically.
Call . . . fortune i.e. fortune favours fools – proverbial.
poke Pocket.
lack-lustre Resigned.
wags Moves on.
moral Moralize.
chanticleer Cockerel.
deep-contemplative Seriously thoughtful.
sans intermission i.e. without a pause.
the only wear The only garb worth wearing.

the gift to know it i.e. they know that they are attractive.

dry Barren, witless.

remainder biscuit This is a reference to the leftover biscuits carried by ships on long voyages instead of bread.

vents Utters in pieces.

suit A pun on (a) request and (b) clothing.

weed A pun picking up and continuing his previous pun.

rank Profusely.

Withal Furthermore.

as large a charter As much freedom.

so fools have i.e. because they are fools they say and do anything.

The why . . . parish church The reason is obvious, like the well-trodden path to a church.

He . . . hit i.e. the target of the mockery.

smart Suffers.

seem senseless of the bob (Not) appear to notice the blow.

If not i.e. if he doesn't do that (appear not to notice).

anatomiz'd Laid open in detail (see note p.19).

squand'ring glances Wandering blows.

Invest Dress, often with the sense of providing the clothes for someone in a particular position.

Cleanse the foul body i.e. purge the corruption.

If they will patiently i.e. if they will listen to me (and notice the disease/medicine imagery).

counter A pun on (a) token, i.e. a wager in name only and (b) parry, a fencing term, preparing for a reply.

chiding Rebuking (it would be a sin for you to rebuke sin in other people).

libertine A person unrestrained by morality.

brutish sting Mating urge.

headed i.e. grown to a head, like a boil. 'sores' and 'evils' refer both to sexually transmitted diseases and more generally to the moral sickness of society.

licence of free foot i.e. with a free hand.

who cries out on pride Is there anyone who criticizes vanity.

tax any private party! Accuse any individual.

Doth . . . ebb? i.e. is it not increasing rapidly to the point where the basic wealth is being used up and not just the interest from it?

bears . . . princes Wears clothes as expensive as those worn by royalty.

basest function Humblest occupation.

bravery . . . cost Expensive clothes not bought by me, and therefore not my concern.

suits Matches, with a pun on 'clothes'.

mettle Spirit, essential meaning.

right justice.

free i.e. from blame.

taxing Criticism.
Unclaimed . . . any man Belonging to no one.
Forbear Stop what you are doing.
Of what kind should . . . What have we here?
touch'd my vein This is a fencing metaphor, meaning 'hit the mark'.
ta'en from me the show i.e. removed the appearance.
inland bred i.e. from a cultivated area (the opposite 'outlandish' is still used today).
nurture Good upbringing.
affairs are answered Needs are supplied.
gentleness . . . i.e. nobility, peacefulness (rather than using force) will make us behave well to you.
had been i.e. would have been.
countenance i.e. appearance.
stern commandment Strict authority.
neglect Pay little attention to.
enforcement Recommendation.
In the which hope . . . i.e. hoping that this will be . . .
engender'd Given rise to.
upon command With our permission.
wanting Need.
minister'd Supplied.
Whiles Until.
suffic'd Satisfied.
oppress'd . . . evils Overcome by weakness.
waste Eat.
all alone unhappy Alone in our unhappiness.
This wide and universal theatre . . . i.e. the world, but note the ironic reference to the play itself, which provides Jaques with a lead in to his famous imaginative definition.
pageants Spectacles, shows.
All the world's a stage Equivalent to the Latin motto of the newly-opened Globe theatre in Shakespeare's time.
Mewling Crying like a cat.
like furnace With passion.
woeful ballad . . . A reference to the contemporary practice of composing poems in praise of trivial aspects of the loved one.
strange oaths Unfamiliar expressions used in swearing.
bearded like the pard Perhaps means ferocious like a leopard, though 'bearded' also means antagonized.
Jealous in honour i.e. sensitive about his reputation.
sudden Decisive.
bubble reputation Passing glory.
justice Magistrate.
capon Traditionally used to bribe magistrates.
formal Precise.
saws Traditional sayings.

modern instances Contemporary examples.
shifts Changes scene.
pantaloon Old fool. This is from the stock character in Italian comedy of the foolish old man in slippers, knee-breeches and spectacles.
pouch Bag or outside pocket.
well sav'd Carefully preserved.
shank Leg.
fall to Set to work, eat.
unkind (a) cruel (b) unnatural.
keen Sharp.
rude Rough.
feigning (a) pretence (b) a pun on 'faining' – longing.
nigh Near.
warp Change to ice.
faithfully In confidence.
effigies witness Likeness see clearly.
limn'd Portrayed.
residue . . . fortune Rest of the story of what has happened to you.
understand i.e. come to learn.

Revision questions on Act II

1 How do changes of scene in this act affect the dramatic action of the play?
2 Compare the characters of Jaques and Duke Senior as they are shown in this act.
3 Write an essay on Shakespeare's use of contrast in Act II.
4 In what ways do you find Jaques an interesting character? Refer to the text closely in your answer.

Act III Scene 1

A brief scene, in which Duke Frederick upbraids Oliver, seizes his lands, and orders him to find Orlando. Oliver says that he has never loved his brother, and is condemned by the Duke for this.

Commentary

A functional scene, but interestingly, in the Duke's condemnation of Oliver, there is some hint of his recognition of wrong in himself – after all, he has banished his own brother – and a hint too of his coming repentance.

the better part made mercy Fundamentally merciful.
absent argument i.e. Orlando.
thou present You being here.
Seek him with candle Look in every corner.
turn Return.
Worth seizure Having any value for us to take.
quit Acquit.
thy brother's mouth i.e. (until he) is here to answer the charge
  himself.
villain See note p.30.
of such a nature i.e. appointed for this sort of work.
make an extent Value and seize until the conditions are met.
expediently Promptly.
turn him going Send him on his way.

Act III Scene 2

Orlando is expressing his love for Rosalind in verses which he
hangs on trees. Meanwhile Touchstone and Corin exchange
views on life, with Touchstone lording it over Corin and his
rustic ways. Each expresses contrasting views which reflect the
differences between court and country. Rosalind enters reading
some of the verses written for her, and Touchstone parodies
them. Celia arrives with more verses in praise of Rosalind, very
extravagant in their comparisons, and the two girls discuss these,
with Celia revealing that Orlando is the author. Rosalind reacts
throughout tremulously, asking Celia where she saw him, and
then finds herself (disguised as Ganymede) facing Orlando, who
enters with Jaques. The latter has been satirically mocking
Orlando's verses to Rosalind, and he and Orlando part, address-
ing each other as 'Signior Love' and 'Signior Melancholy' respectively. Rosalind daringly engages Orlando in conversation
(obviously he doesn't recognize her), and he reveals that he is the
one who is 'so love-shaked'. Rosalind describes love as a 'madness', but says that she will help cure Orlando of his love if he
will come to court her every day in the name of 'Rosalind'. This
Orlando agrees to do.

Commentary

This long scene brings the lovers together, is full of dramatic
irony (since Orlando does not know Rosalind but agrees in effect
to court her), so that the mock wooing provides a running

humorous innuendo for the audience. Orlando's verses epito-
mize romantic love, and here Shakespeare may be mocking the
excesses of some of his contemporaries. The dialogue between
Touchstone and Corin demonstrates the former's high opinion
of himself and shows his capacity for wit and word-play. The
exchange demonstrates that he is no 'fool'. Corin reveals that he
is a 'true labourer', totally at variance with Touchstone's court
wit, but able to answer him with his homely philosophy and
honesty. There is also a forthrightness about him that compares
with the banished Duke's appreciation of nature and true morality in this lower sphere of society.

There is a delicious comedy sequence as Rosalind reads the
verses to herself and Touchstone coarsely but brilliantly parodies them. Note the movement from prose among the lower
characters to lyrical verse as the romance theme becomes dominant. Note also the word-play between Rosalind and Touchstone, with each scoring off the other. The verses read by Celia
underpin the romantic element but are also a balance to 'All the
world's a stage', since they too are pronouncing on life. They
constitute a fine hyperbole of Rosalind's characteristics through
a range of classical love references. Rosalind at first responds
coolly though wittily, but Celia keeps her on tenterhooks. The
dramatic excitement of the scene with Rosalind's tremulousness
and Celia's enjoyment of her own role and news, is heightened
by the arrival of Orlando and Jaques. Here again the contrast
between the two men is effectively employed, Jaques's cynicism
and Orlando's romantic excess neatly balancing each other.
Rosalind's courage, verve, wit and ingenuity are shown when she
nerves herself to speak to Orlando, with the running commentary of her mistaken identity adding to the audience's
enjoyment of the play. After the romantic verse we are in colloquial prose again, with Rosalind mistress of the verbal innuendo
and associations. She cunningly gets around to the subject of the
carving of her name on the barks of trees, and brilliantly sat-
irizes the conventional manifestations of being love-lorn.
Rosalind's plan ensures that the temperature of both humour
and romance will remain high, since she is establishing Orlando's courtship. The whole of the mock-wooing sequence is
redolent of dramatic irony. We might also note that Rosalind has
taken over the action, and that Celia, who has been so witty and
central to the action, has been eclipsed. The main emphasis of

the romance is on the deception of the Rosalind/Orlando make-believe.

thrice-crowned queen of night The moon-goddess had three forms representing heaven, earth and hell respectively.
pale sphere i.e. the moon.
huntress Diana, the moon goddess on earth, was a huntress and protected maidens. The reference here is to Rosalind, who is pure and therefore serves the goddess.
full Whole.
sway Control.
character Inscribe, write.
witness'd i.e. borne witness to.
unexpressive i.e. inexpressible, too beautiful to be described.
private Solitary.
spare Comfortless.
humour Temperament.
more plenty i.e. enough food.
means Resources.
by nature nor art i.e. either from his birth or from what he has learned.
may complain Bewail the lack of.
kindred Family strain.
a natural philosopher A pun meaning (a) naturally wise and (b) idiotically wise.
court i.e. the court, aristocratic society.
Nay, I hope I hope not.
parlous Dangerous.
Not a whit Not in the least.
manners i.e. way of life and behaviour.
salute Greet.
that courtesy would be uncleanly . . . i.e. if kissing of hands were practised in the country, we would be kissing the dirtiness and smells (of the shepherds).
Instance Give an example.
still Continually.
fells Fleeces.
sounder i.e. better.
tarred over Stained.
surgery i.e. treatment of injuries and disease.
tar This was used as an ointment.
civet A cat, the secretions from its glands being used as a perfume base to which essences are added.
worms-meat i.e. only fit as food for worms.
perpend Consider, weigh it carefully.
baser birth Lower origin.
flux Discharge.

Mend the instance i.e. give us a better example (than this one).

incision Cut, the idea being to cure his rawness.

raw A pun on (a) lacking experience and (b) uncooked.

content with my harm i.e. put up with that I have to suffer.

cattle Livestock generally.

bawd to a bell-wether i.e. procuring mates for the leader of the flock, which wore a bell round its neck.

betray i.e. allow to be mated by.

crooked-pated Twisted horns, indicative of great age.

cuckoldly Having horns (the symbol of betrayal of a man by a woman).

reasonable match Suitable mating.

Inde i.e. Indies.

mounted i.e. carried by (the implication being that her beauty is known everywhere).

lin'd Drawn.

black to i.e. are very poor (in comparison to Rosalind).

fair Beauty.

I'll rhyme . . . together I could go on making rhymes like that (for eight consecutive years).

the right butter-women's rank to market i.e. the rhymes gallop along behind one another like a row of butter-women riding to market.

Out Get away with you.

taste Start.

after kind i.e. its own species.

Winter'd i.e. used in winter.

lin'd Stuffed (with a sexual pun), mated.

to cart i.e. take her away, just as sheaves and prostitutes were tied to carts.

rose (a) flower (b) a beautiful woman (c) the female sexual organ.

prick (a) thorn (b) the mark of Cupid's arrow (c) the male sexual organ.

false gallop i.e. continuing the image, here meaning 'wrong rhythm'.

infect Affect.

graff graft Cross.

medlar A small brown-skinned fruit, only eaten when slightly decayed, with a pun on 'meddler' – one who interferes.

property Virtue.

Tongues i.e. writings.

civil sayings Rational comments

erring Wandering.

stretching . . . span (a) handsbreath (b) the short life of man.

Buckles in his sum of age i.e. confines him to his lifetime.

violated vows Broken promises.

quintessence The purest, finest part.

sprite Soul.

little Miniature (Rosalind is the emblem of perfection).

charg'd Instructed.

wide-enlarg'd i.e. gathered from far and wide.

Helen's cheek . . . A reference to the legendary Helen of Troy, whose beauty caused the Greeks to besiege Troy for her return.

Cleopatra's Cleopatra, queen of Egypt, successively mistress of Julius Caesar and Mark Antony.

Atalanta's better part Atalanta maintained her chastity by outrunning her suitors.

Sad Lucretia's modesty Noble Lucretia was a Roman matron who committed suicide rather than give up her honour.

of many parts Having great beauty, talent, virtue, the noble graces.

synod Assembly.

touches (a) traits (b) brush-strokes, as in a painting.

would Willed.

tedious homily Boring lecture.

withal With.

sirrah Sir, but spoken with authority.

scrip and scrippage An expression to parallel 'bag and baggage'. A scrip was a small bag carried by poor people.

feet . . . bear An extended metaphor, punning on the metrical 'feet' of poetry and 'feet and legs', as well as 'bear' meaning stand, put up with and carry.

seven of the nine days A wonder was supposed to last for nine days, hence the phrase 'a nine days' wonder' implying that people soon get used to even the most miraculous things. Rosalind has nearly got over this 'wonder'.

berhymed i.e. had so many rhymes (written about me).

Pythagoras Greek philosopher who expounded the theory that the soul, after the death of the body, could enter another person or animal.

that When.

an Irish rat The Elizabethans made fun of the Irish belief that chanting verses could be used to kill. This was supposed to be how the rats in Ireland were wiped out.

Trow you Can you imagine.

Change your colour? Presumably, Rosalind is blushing.

friends . . . encounter A reversal of the usual proverb 'Friends may meet but mountains may not greet', meaning that friends can be flexible and approach each other. Celia is saying here that Rosalind is being stubborn and that it is easier to move mountains than to make her understand.

petitionary vehemence Strong begging.

out . . . whooping Beyond all expression of excitement.

Good my complexion! A mild oath like 'my goodness'.

caparisoned Decked out, dressed.

doublet and hose in my disposition i.e. that I have the temperament of a man.

a South Sea of discovery i.e. take as long as a voyage to the South Seas.

apace Quickly.

concealed i.e. secret.

a man in your belly Celia is playing on Rosalind having her lover sexually, and on her becoming pregnant too.

of God's making i.e. real, not a figment of the imagination.

thankful Worthy.

stay Wait for.

sad brow and true maid i.e. tell me seriously and truthfully.

I'faith Truly.

Wherein went he? What was he dressed like?

What makes he here? What is he doing?

Gargantua The giant with the large mouth in the story by the French writer Rabelais (1494–1553).

this age's size i.e. nowadays.

particulars i.e. particular questions.

catechism Course of questions.

freshly Attractive.

atomies Minute particles.

resolve the propositions Completely answer the queries.

taste . . . relish i.e. enjoy what I have told you.

good observance Careful note.

Jove's tree i.e. an oak, sacred to Jove.

well becomes the ground Improves the appearance of the earth.

holla Stop.

curvets unseasonably Frisks about uncomfortably (like a horse).

heart (a) Rosalind's heart (b) the hart sought by the hunter.

burden Punning still, meaning (a) without a weight (b) chorus.

fashion Normal politeness.

society Company.

God buy you God be with you – the modern 'Goodbye'.

better strangers i.e. not meet at all (because both of them want to be alone).

just i.e. that's right.

as high as my heart Probably a romantic answer, since the reality would make Rosalind rather short!

pretty Clever.

goldsmiths' wives i.e. women who would have seen many gold rings with sentimental mottoes engraved on them.

conned Memorized.

out of rings i.e. from the rings.

right . . . cloth The usual cheap imitation of tapestry.

breather Man.

By my troth i.e. in all honesty.

seeking for a fool i.e. Touchstone.

drowned in the brook This is a set joke about seeing one's own reflection.

figure (a) likeness (b) number. Jaques means the first, Orlando means both.

cipher Arithmetical symbol for nothing.
under that habit By that deception.
play the knave with i.e. trick.
detect Reveal.
the lazy foot The slow passage.
proper Accurate.
divers Various.
se'nnight i.e. a week.
hard Slow.
wasteful i.e. causing the body to waste away.
softly Slowly.
term Period into which the Law Courts divide their year.
cony Rabbit.
kindled Born.
purchase Acquire.
courtship A pun on (a) the business of the court and (b) the act of wooing.
touched Tainted.
giddy Silly, frivolous.
taxed Accused.
physic Remedy.
odes Poetic addresses.
elegies Poems of lamentation.
deifying i.e. making a goddess of.
fancy-monger Dealer in fantasy.
quotidian A fever.
love-shaked A continuation of the metaphor above – shaking with the ague or fever.
blue eye i.e. dark-ringed.
unquestionable Unreasonable.
unbanded i.e. having no hat-band.
careless desolation Lack of concern about your own comfort.
point-device Scrupulously correct.
as loving yourself i.e. putting yourself first.
a dark house and a whip i.e. the Elizabethan treatment for those who were thought to be mad.
ordinary Common.
profess Claim the ability to.
moonish Changeable.
fantastical Full of imaginary whims.
apish Foolishly imitative.
for every passion . . . anything Unpredictable.
entertain Show kindness to.
forswear Reject.
drave Drove.
mad . . . madness i.e. from being madly in love to being actually insane.

liver Considered to be the seat of love and ardent passion.
clean . . . sheep's heart Sheep were supposed to be devoid of feelings.

Act III Scene 3

Touchstone has found his own consolation in meeting a country wench Audrey, though Jaques is watching their exchanges. Touchstone discusses poetry, which is well above Audrey's head, and reveals that he has already arranged for them to be married. He also expatiates upon marriage despite the risk of being cuckolded; he has arranged with Sir Oliver Martext, a priest, to be married, although of course this may not be legal. In other words, he hopes to arrange a marriage which will delude Audrey. Jaques intervenes, and the marriage is postponed.

Commentary

This scene effectively introduces the sub-plot involving Touchstone and Audrey. Jaques's moralizing provides a softer note – he wants a proper marriage or nothing for Touchstone and Audrey – whilst a darker side of Touchstone's character is revealed – he wants Audrey for his mistress. There are satirical shafts at poetry, at marriage, at adultery, but the main comic interaction is twofold: (a) the observation and intervention of Jaques and (b) Audrey's lack of comprehension of the 'fool' she is about to 'marry'. Sir Oliver Martext is pure caricature, intent on conning the simple into believing that he has some status.

feature General appearance.
capricious Literally, goat-like and therefore lustful. Contradicted by 'honest'.
Ovid The Roman love poet was banished by Augustus in AD 8, and thereafter lived on the Black Sea among the barbarians. Note the humour in Touchstone likening his own position to that of the cultured Latin poet.
Goths i.e. barbarians.
ill-inhabited Misplaced.
seconded i.e. supported (by being understood).
a great reckoning . . . room A bill in payment for lodging at a disreputable inn.
hard-favoured Of unpleasing appearance, ugly.
honey a sauce to sugar i.e. too much of a good thing.
material Self-important.

Sir Oliver Martext Note the use of 'mar' – spoil. 'Sir' was a title of respect given to clergymen in Shakespeare's day.
couple i.e. join in marriage.
fain Wish to.
stagger i.e. hesitate.
temple . . . assembly Church . . . congregation.
no end of his goods i.e. (doesn't know) that he has so much.
no end of them i.e. he is constantly betrayed.
noblest deer . . . rascal The young buck and the villain alike (are equally likely to be betrayed).
forehead i.e. where the horns are carried.
defence i.e. a fencing metaphor, but also cleverly linked to 'walled'.
dispatch Deal with.
on gift of any man i.e. after some man has used her and wants to give her away.
God 'ild you God repay you.
last company Previous action.
toy Trifle.
be covered Put your hat on.
bow Yoke.
curb Bit.
bells These were attached to the hawk's leg, so that the falconer could hear where the bird was.
bill i.e. rub their beaks together when courting.
wedlock would be nibbling Marriage would be a steady tasting.
wainscot Wooden panelling.
warp (a) twist as in timber (b) turn from correct behaviour.
I am not in the mind I don't really feel like.
well Correctly, properly (in church).
bawdry i.e. live immorally.
O sweet Oliver This was a popular song at the time.
Wind Go, proceed.
fantastical Eccentric.
flout me out of my calling i.e. mock me out of my living.

Act III Scene 4

Rosalind is fretting to Celia about the non-arrival of Orlando to woo his 'Rosalind'. Celia maintains her teasing role, and it is revealed that Rosalind has met the banished Duke, in reality her father, and that he too has not seen through her disguise. Corin enters while they are talking and urges them to watch the 'pageant' of the rustic lovers Sylvius and Phebe.

Commentary

This scene shows the urgency of Rosalind's love – she is pining for Orlando's arrival – and Celia uses the opportunity not only to tease but to question Orlando's sincerity, or at least his sincerity towards this 'Rosalind'. The mistaken identity theme is further underlined by the banished Duke's failure to recognize his own daughter. And indeed Rosalind's obsession with Orlando is given emphasis in her decision to hide her identity from her father. The Sylvius/Phebe sub-plot again makes us aware of the structure of the play centering, as it does, on the various lovers and their adventures and misadventures in love.

dissembling Deceiving.
Judas's Judas Iscariot, the betrayer of Christ, is often depicted with red or auburn hair.
Judas's own children i.e. false and treacherous.
Your chestnut i.e. the one everybody recognizes.
cast lips of Diana i.e. modelled on those of the goddess of chastity.
winter's sisterhood i.e. of the utmost frigidity.
concave Hollow.
tapster One who draws the ale in a tavern.
confirmer of false reckonings i.e. giving dishonest bills.
question Talk.
quite traverse i.e. right across, completely.
athwart Across.
puisny tilter A poor jouster at a tournament, obviously not one of the main attractions.
but on one side i.e. avoiding the main encounter.
goose Coward.
pageant Performance.
will mark it Want to see it.
remove Leave. Note the rounding off of the scene in rhyming couplets.
a busy actor Note the stage metaphor, and also that Rosalind, ever spirited, intends to take part in the confrontation.

Act III Scene 5

Silvius is bemoaning Phebe's disdainful rejection of him. Phebe says that she only wishes to escape from his attentions, while Silvius tells her that she too may suffer from the pangs of unrequited love. Rosalind enters and berates Phebe in no uncertain terms for her hard-heartedness. She also gives her some good advice 'sell when you can, you are not for all markets' but Phebe encourages her to talk on.

Rosalind notes Phebe's immediate and wonder-struck reponse to her (Rosalind) and urges Phebe not to fall in love with her. After Rosalind has gone Phebe shares her suffering in love with Silvius. In a long closing speech which is full of contradictions about her own state of mind, Phebe reveals her obsession for Rosalind, and tells Silvius that she will write a letter to Rosalind, which Silvius shall take to her.

Commentary

All the conventions of pastoral love appear in the dialogue between Silvius and Phebe, but the main effect is to further complicate the plot, for here we have a girl (Phebe) falling in love with a girl (Rosalind) who appears to be a man. The language however transcends the pastoral convention, with references to murder and execution, while the love-at-first-sight theme is reinforced by the reference to Marlowe and to eyes. The irony is immediate and dramatic, for Phebe disdainful is transformed into Phebe suddenly in love. Rosalind is outspoken to Phebe, a subtle underlining of her anxiety because she has not seen Orlando. Her bluntness has the earthy quality of real irritation, and we notice that she is beginning to command the action. Her outspokenness does not hide the truth despite her disguise, and she provides tantalizing hints that she is not what she appears ('I am falser than vows made in wine'), thus adding to the dramatic irony of the scene as well as emphasizing the mistaken identity motif of the play. The structural awareness is again evident, since Phebe in her sighs of love is now in the same position as Rosalind sighing for Orlando. Natural imagery is used ironically to indicate the purity of Silvius's love, but we should not underrate the effect of this sub-plot; Phebe's speech in which she alternately denies feeling anything for Rosalind and yet allows her every utterance to confirm that she is in love, is one of the finest in the play. The see-sawing movement of the verse is echoed in the thoughts and the emotions, thus showing Shakespeare's ability to bring an unlikely character to life through the suddenness of her dilemma. The softening of Phebe to Silvius also indicates her capacity to accept him ultimately. Note that the whole scene is in blank verse, suitable to the romantic sentiments and the pastoral convention.

Falls Makes to fall.

begs pardon i.e. apologizes (for what he has to do).

shut . . . atomies Close their eyelids against atoms, minute specks.

counterfeit Pretend.

cicatrice A mark like a scar.

capable impressure i.e. the impression it leaves.

cheek Face.

fancy Love.

wounds invisible i.e. sufferings.

love's keen arrows i.e. shot by Cupid.

Afflict . . . mocks i.e. laugh at me.

mother i.e. who should have taught you better.

no beauty No great beauty.

without candle . . . to bed i.e. you would only be taken to bed if it were too dark to see what you looked like.

ordinary . . . sale-work (you are) a common commodity.

'Od's my little life A corruption of 'May God save my little life'.

tangle Ensnare.

bugle i.e. like black glass beads.

foggy South The wind bringing warmth and rain, suggesting hot breath.

properer Better-looking.

glass Mirror.

proper Attractive.

lineaments Features.

fasting i.e. in penance.

Sell . . . markets Take whatever offer you can get, for you won't appeal to everyone.

Cry the man mercy Beg forgiveness.

Foul is most foul . . . scoffer Scornful behaviour on top of ugliness is the worst combination.

a year together For a whole year long.

vows made in wine i.e. promises made when one is drunk.

tuft . . . hard by i.e. grove of olive trees near here.

ply Press.

better In a more kindly way.

abus'd Deceived (in his judgment).

Dead shepherd The address is to and the quotation from Shakespeare's great contemporary, Christopher Marlowe (1564–93). It was a pastoral convention to refer to a poet as a 'shepherd', and Marlowe had written the well-known lyric *The Passionate Shepherd to his Love*.

saw See note p.39.

'Who ever lov'd . . . sight?' The quotation is from Marlowe's *Hero and Leander* published posthumously in 1598.
erst Formerly.
poverty of grace i.e. lack of happiness.
glean . . . reaps i.e. have what someone else leaves.
Loose Release.
scatter'd Occasional.
erewhile A short time ago.
bounds Territory.
carlot Peasant.
peevish Mischief-making.
proper Handsome.
complexion Appearance.
mingled damask Mixed red and white (as roses).
In parcels Casually.
For what had he to do . . . i.e. what right had he . . .
am remember'd Recall.
that's all one It's all the same to me.
Omittance is no quittance (Because I) don't do something now, doesn't mean that I won't do it in the future.
straight Now.
passing short Very brief and rude.

Revisions questions on Act III

1 Indicate the nature of Rosalind's development as a character in this act.
2 How important dramatically are the Touchstone/Audrey and Silvius/Phebe sub-plots?
3 Discuss the dramatic importance of Act III Scene 2.
4 Write an essay on the variety of language used in this act.
5 Comment on the effects of mistaken identity in this act.

Act IV Scene 1

Jaques boasts to Rosalind of the unique quality of his melancholy derived from his travels. Her exchange with Jaques is as we should expect witty, but the arrival of Orlando sees her reprimanding him for his lateness. Orlando proceeds to woo his 'Rosalind', with much encouragement and teasing from her. She gives him a lecture in order to demonstrate that men do not die for love. Celia performs a mock-marriage between them. Orlando promises to return after two hours, and Celia tells Rosalind off for abusing her sex.

Commentary

The scene is virtually dominated by Rosalind. Jaques continues
to indulge his fancy and his wit, but Rosalind is equal to them
both, and responds by drawing the nature-court analogy so
common in this play. She also has some telling comments on the
way travellers disparage their own country when they return to
it. We are constantly amazed now by her intelligence and her
grasp. Orlando is virtually reduced to brief answers to her brilliant word-play, fancies and verve, for Rosalind can develop an
analogy (note the one with the snail). Clearly she is enjoying the
situation of having – yet not having – her lover. She ransacks
classical allusions in order to demonstrate her point that men do
not die for love. Celia rarely gets in a word, but note again that
structurally this mock-marriage is an echo of the one Touchstone contemplated with Audrey. The humour lies of course in
the dramatic irony and the mistaken identity, but Rosalind's
sense of reality is never far away – note how she defines the
nature of romance and reality, the changes in people towards
each other once they are married. For all her fantasy, Rosalind's
feet are on the ground. She mocks her own state by subtle
references, but confesses herself to Celia, and we respect the
depth of her feeling for Orlando. Her wit is a cover for its
genuineness. Her wish to be alone indicates her anxiety, but it is
self-indulgent too, and might be compared with the indulgence
of Jaques. Note that this scene is in prose, contrasting with the
previous scene, with its pastoral poetry.

in extremity of i.e. given to the extreme (of laughter or sadness).
emulaton The wish to copy someone superior.
fantas*t*ical Arising solely from the imagination.
politic Cunning, calculating.
nice Over-refined.
sundry contemplation Various results.
often rumination Frequent thinking.
talk in blank verse Note the mockery here, almost as if Shakespeare is
  sending up through Jaques his own practice!
Monsieur Traveller Rosalind is satirizing the affectations of travellers
  who have returned and have much to tell.
lisp Put on an accent.
disable Run down.
nativity i.e. native land.
countenance Appearance.

swam in a gondola i.e. been to Venice.

serve me such another trick i.e. stay away again.

clapped him o' th' shoulder Touched him slightly.

warrant him heart-whole Guarantee that he has not lost his heart to anyone.

jointure i.e. the arrangement whereby the woman becomes joint owner, perhaps part of the marriage arrangements.

horns Rosalind is playing on the term, implying a cuckolded man.

fain to be beholding . . . Bound to expect from your wives

armed in his fortune i.e. having already (the horns).

leer Appearance.

holiday humour Light-hearted mood.

like enough Almost certain.

and If.

gravelled . . . matter i.e. found that you couldn't say anything.

cleanliest shift Clearest course.

puts you to entreaty Makes you beg.

ranker Stronger, more overpowering.

suit (a) proposition (b) clothes.

by attorney Using a deputy or substitute.

videlicet Latin for 'that is to say'.

Troilus . . . Grecian club Troilus, the Trojan prince, was heartbroken by Cressida's faithlessness, and was eventually killed in battle by Achilles. The story of these lovers provided Chaucer with a long narrative poem and Shakespeare with the basic material for his play *Troilus and Cressida*. Rosalind is emphasizing that men do not die of love.

Leander In classical mythology, he tried to swim the Hellespont to see Hero, but was drowned in a storm.

found Decided.

right Real.

coming-on disposition Encouraging way.

commission Authority.

goes before the priest i.e. makes her responses before the priest asks her.

possessed Got.

April . . . December i.e. passionate when they woo, but afterwards cold.

Maids . . . wives Rosalind actually says that the same is true of women – they are at first romantic, but 'the sky changes' – things alter after marriage.

Barbary cock-pigeon Traditionally quoted as an example of jealousy, Barbary being North Africa.

against rain Before rain.

new-fangled Fascinated by new things.

giddy in my desires Unpredictable.

Diana in the fountain Statues from classical mythology were a commonplace in Shakespeare's London, but this reference seems to derive from the name of the heroine of a Portuguese pastoral play.

hyen Hyena.

waywarder More difficult.

Make the Shut.

out at the casement Leave by the window.

'Wit, whither wilt?' Popular expression of the time, used to stop excessive chattering.

check Means of stopping (the flow of language).

And what wit . . . excuse that? And how would you explain away such behaviour?

occasion Doing fault.

what you would prove i.e. how you would behave.

'Tis but one cast away i.e. I am forsaken.

mend me Correct me (if I'm not sincere).

not dangerous Not blasphemous.

pathetical Pitiful.

hollow Worthless, shallow.

religion Sincerity.

justice i.e. magistrate.

let Time try Let time be the judge.

simply misused Thoroughly abused.

love-prate Love talk.

doublet . . . head i.e. unmask you, reveal who you are.

sounded Measured.

Bay of Portugal A reference to the fact that the sea is very deep off Oporto.

bastard of Venus i.e. Cupid, whose father was Mercury not Vulcan, Venus's real husband.

spleen Impulse.

a shadow A sheltered place.

Act IV Scene 2

This is a musical interlude, with a song about the killing of the deer.

Commentary

The forest atmosphere of the play is maintained by the song, though prior to this Jaques waxes briefly satirical, comparing the successful hunter to a Roman conqueror. The song itself has a ruining innuendo about 'horns' and 'burden' which suggests cuckolding, and almost captures Jaques's own cynical tone. The scene is obviously functional, the interlude marking the passage of time.

like a Roman conqueror i.e. in his triumph, as if he had returned to Rome, his victories being celebrated by garlanding and procession.

bear/This burden (a) wear the horns of a cuckold (b) carry the carcass of the deer (c) sing the chorus.

crest Heraldic device about the shield and helmet on a coat of arms.

Act IV Scene 3

Rosalind is anxious that Orlando has not turned up at his appointed time. Silvius enters bearing the note from Phebe to Rosalind, obviously innocent of its contents. Rosalind at first suspects or affects to suspect that the letter has been written by Silvius. She reads it to Silvius who is hardly able to understand it; the letter is Phebe's confession of love for Rosalind. The latter sends Silvius back to order Phebe to love him (Silvius). Oliver enters dramatically, and narrates how Orlando has saved him from a lion. He gives Rosalind the bloody napkin, and tells her and Celia that he is Orlando's brother, and that he has tried to kill him. Orlando had taken Oliver to the Duke, and after that to his cave, where he displayed the wound he had received from the lion, and fainted away calling upon 'his Rosalind'. Rosalind herself faints at this news, but rallies and says how she has 'counterfeited' her reaction. Oliver does not believe this, but Rosalind, though shaken, says that he must go to tell Orlando what he has seen.

Commentary

Again we note the variety in this scene. Silvius is easily duped, but Rosalind determines that the truth will out, and in reading the letter brings it home to Silvius. The prose of her indictment of Phebe contrasts with the lyrical 'railing' of the letter. However, before the mistaken identity theme can be further developed the entrance of Oliver heightens the dramatic atmosphere and prepares for the ultimate theme of repentance and reconciliation. Note the wildness of the natural setting – the snake and the lion, which shows that nature has her predators, just as courts have. The emphasis is on the inherent goodness of human nature, which causes Orlando to rescue his hitherto evil brother at great risk to himself, and causes that brother to repent. We note the dramatic tension of Oliver's story and of his confession. Even better dramatically is Rosalind's swoon, genuine but, because of her disguise, unaccountable. There is some superb word-play (note the use of 'counterfeit') but the humour of the mistaken identity situation is now underlined with pathos. Rosalind cannot help revealing herself for what she is by her reaction, and we also note that Celia, subordinate for so long, keeps her head in this crisis.

here much Orlando Rosalind is being very sarcastic about the fact that Orlando hasn't turned up.

tenour General sense.

phoenix Mythical bird, only one of which is living at a given time.

device i.e. made up by Silvius.

extremity Extreme behaviour.

leathern i.e. as hard as leather.

freestone-colour'd Sandy-grey.

hussif's Properly housewife's, but indicating a lower status – housemaid's.

Ethiop Ethiopian i.e. black.

blacker . . . countenance Worse in their meaning than in their appearance.

godhead Divine nature.

laid apart Set aside.

Warr'st Battle, fight.

eyne Eyes.

Alack Alas.

mild aspect i.e. if they looked kindly (on me).

He i.e. Silvius.

by him Having used him as a messenger.

seal up thy mind Put your response in a sealed letter.

kind Nature.

all that I can make Everything that I can offer.

charge Order.

hence Go away.

purlieus i.e. cultivated glades.

neighbour bottom Nearby hollow.

rank of osiers Row of willows.

left on your right hand i.e. to the left behind you.

favour Look, appearance.

bestows himself Behaves.

ripe sister Grown girl.

low Short.

browner Darker-haired, or perhaps with more umber on her face.

commend him Sends his greetings.

napkin Handkerchief.

sweet and bitter fancy i.e. thinking of his love.

bald Leafless.
dry antiquity Old age.
gilded Gold-coloured.
nimble in threats Darting menacingly.
indented i.e. leaving marks behind as it curved away.
udders all drawn dry i.e. lacking nourishment.
When that Until.
disposition Nature.
render Portray.
purpos'd so Intended to do so.
kindness Family loyalty.
occasion Opportunity.
in which hurtling During this commotion.
being the thing I am What I am now.
By and by i.e. I'll come to that in a minute.
Tears our recountments i.e. we wept as we told each other our adventures.
array and entertainment Clothes and food.
recover'd Revived.
counterfeited See note p.52.
testimony in your complexion Evidence in your pallor.
passion of earnest Genuine emotion.
draw Drag (yourself).
excuse Forgive.

Revision questions on Act IV

1 Write an essay on the range of Rosalind's wit in this act.
2 What gain is there in dramatic effect by having Orlando's rescue by Oliver described instead of being enacted on stage?
3 Show how the theme of mistaken identity is used to positive dramatic effect in this act.
4 In what ways does this act lack realism? Choose certain characters and say in what way they fail to convince us of their credibility.
5 Write an essay on the use of different kinds of verse and song in this act.

Act V Scene 1

William, Touchstone's rival for the affections of Audrey, appears. He is fair game for Touchstone's wit, and is summarily packed off by him with threats which he doesn't understand.

Commentary

This seems an unnecessary scene, since it merely provides Touchstone with the opportunity of displaying his courtier's wit at the expense of the simple-minded rustic. Touchstone has a nice line in threats and boasting.

It is meat and drink . . . Note the irony of this.
flouting Making fun.
hold Contain ourselves.
Cover thy head William has taken his cap off as a sign of respect.
To have is to have Equivalent to our 'possession is nine-tenths of the law'.
figure in rhetoric Concept in formal logical argument.
ipse Himself (Latin).
the vulgar i.e. the vulgar tongue – colloquial.
in bastinado With a cudgel.
in steel With a sword.
faction Argument.

Act V Scene 2

We learn from the conversation between Orlando and Oliver that the latter has fallen in love with Celia. If Orlando approves, Oliver will settle his lands upon him as recompense for his past actions. Rosalind appears to comfort Orlando and to explain her counterfeiting. She also dwells on Celia's love for Oliver. Orlando says that his brother and Celia will be married the next day, but bemoans the fact that he cannot marry his Rosalind. The latter says that she can produce Rosalind by magic the next day, and that Orlando shall have her. Meanwhile Phebe enters with Silvius, accusing Rosalind of having betrayed her by reading the letter to Silvius. There follows a chorus from each of the lovers naming their true loves and describing the nature of their love. They end by arguing, but Rosalind tells them in effect, though with much word-play, that all will be set right by her the next day.

Commentary

Two themes, those of love at first sight and reconciliation, are the mainspring of the first part of this scene, and these give way to Rosalind's brilliant parody of 'I came, I saw, I conquered', her delight in Celia's and Oliver's passion perhaps complemented by her own. All is prepared for the revelations of identity to come, with Rosalind as the worker of magic. The controlled repetition of vows acts as a kind of refrain; and Rosalind's 'And so am I for no woman' acting as a kind of ironic commentary on the theme of mistaken identity which has led them all (except Oliver and Celia) into this love-tangle. The scene of double entendres is initiated and carried through as she prepares for the marriages on the following day. The key as ever is the dramatic irony, for Rosalind has all the power, not by magic but by nature, to bring all things to a happy conclusion.

giddiness Suddenness.
question Doubt.
good Advantage.
estate Bequeath, make over (forgetting that it has been confiscated by Duke Frederick).
greater wonders Even more remarkable things.
where you are What you are thinking.
fight of two rams This is often quoted as an example of aggressiveness.
thrasonical Boastful (literally, like Thraso, a bragging soldier in a play by the Roman dramatist Terence).
degrees Stages, steps (links with 'stairs').
a pair of stairs i.e. a path.
incontinent (a) without delay (b) without restraining their sexual appetites.
wrath Passion.
Clubs A contemporary for keeping order, but perhaps with the idea that violence cannot keep Celia and Oliver apart.
nuptial Wedding.
height of heart-heaviness Depths of depression.
by thinking i.e. by this pretence.
conceit Judgment.
to grace me To do myself justice.
conversed Given some time.
not damnable i.e. did not practise the evil arts of black magic.
so near the heart As strongly.
gesture Behaviour.
cries out Bears witness to.
inconvenient Improper, mischievous.
human i.e. as a human, not an illusion.
danger i.e. of the effects of witchcraft.
in sober meanings i.e. seriously.
bid Invite.
ungentleness Disservice.

study Motive.
despiteful Disdainful.
observance Respect.
howling . . . moon i.e. noisy but pointless.

Act V Scene 3

Touchstone and Audrey prepare for their marriage. However, the scene is really devoted to another of the songs, this one about the pleasures of young love.

Commentary

We note the structural coherence here, for the subject of marriage and celebration is continued by Touchstone and Audrey, and exemplified in another fine song which underlines the major theme of the play, love. It is also a song to spring, the time of the seasons, and thus appropriate to the forest setting, and also to youth, appropriate to the young lovers of the play.

dishonest Immodest.
a woman of the world i.e. to be a married woman, to live life fully.
clap into't roundly i.e. get on with it immediately.
hawking Clearing the throat.
two gipsies on a horse i.e. indistinguishable from each other.
ring-time A time for (a) wedding-bells and (b) dances in a ring.
acres Furrows.
carol (a) merry song and (b) ring-dance with its song.
prime (a) springtime and (b) youthfulness.
untuneable i.e. the wrong tone for innocent young boys, and also out of tune.
mend (a) improve (b) repair (since their voices may be breaking).

Act V Scene 4

The concluding scene of the play, Duke Senior agrees with 'Ganymede' that if 'he' brings in Rosalind he will give her in marriage to Orlando. Phebe agrees to marry Silvius if she can't marry Rosalind. Celia and Rosalind leave and the Duke and Orlando remark that they have seen in Ganymede's looks some resemblance to his (the Duke's) daughter. Audrey and Touchstone appear straight from their marriage service. Touchstone executes a parody of duelling terms to describe the extremes of courtly behaviour, and courtly cowardice. After this exchange Hymen enters with Rosalind and Celia; the Duke recognizes his daughter, Phebe relinquishes her claim, and the marriage masque for the various couples begins. Jaques – the second son of Sir Rowland de Boys – brings news of the usurping Duke Frederick's conversion to the religious life. Jaques – the real Jaques of the play – gives his blessings to the couples, and goes off to see the converted Duke, emphasizing 'I am for other than for dancing measures'. After the celebratory dance, Rosalind speaks as the Epilogue; she has dominated the play, and in a sense it is only right that she should have the last word.

Commentary

Delay in the revelation of 'Ganymede's' identity to the others has increased the audience's suspense. Touchstone's satirical wit occupies attention while Rosalind goes to change. The masque with which the play closes was a combination of music, song and dance, generally designed as part of the festivities on some happy occasion. It was frequently performed in private houses, and was very popular in the late Elizabethan period. There is general agreement that the introduction of Hymen, god of marriage, is somewhat artificial in a play which has been concerned for the most part with real rather than allegorical characters. The masque provides the opportunity for a dance under the greenwood tree, a fitting ending for a romantic comedy of this type. The revelation that Duke Frederick has been converted is another arbitrary note, and this last scene leaves much to be desired both structurally and in terms of the audience's being convinced by the actions. In a sense, Touchstone's satire of courtly behaviour is the finest part of it, because it is of a piece with what has gone before. Even his aside ('Bear your body more seeming, Audrey') shows his deliberate assumption of superiority over the rustics which he has maintained throughout the play. Rosalind is virtually silent throughout the action, but Jaques's determination to visit the repented Duke is typical of his whimsical idea of using odd behaviour as grist to his verbal mill. Rosalind's epilogue somewhat redeems her, though it is largely a homily to account for the title of the play. Only the last few lines show us the real Rosalind, loveable because she has something of

the bitch as well as genuine femininity in her make-up. It is
fitting that she should say 'I would kiss as many of you as had
beards that pleased me' for, despite her love for Orlando, she
never loses her wit, and she is never dull.

fear they hope i.e. are afraid to hope.
they fear i.e. the worst.
our compact is urg'd Our agreement is confirmed.
lively touches . . . favour Living signs . . . appearance.
rudiments Basic principles.
desperate i.e. causing danger.
Obscured Hidden.
toward Approaching.
put me to my purgation Try me and allow me to clear myself.
smooth Seeming friendly.
undone Ruined (the tailors by not settling his accounts with them).
like to have i.e. nearly.
ta'en up Made up.
seventh cause Last degree. See Touchstone's later explanation.
desire you of the like And you too.
copulatives Those about to be married.
swear and forswear Keep and break promises.
breaks i.e. the bride is a virgin.
humour Whimsical idea.
swift and sententious Quick and full of pointed remarks.
fool's bolt i.e. like the missile used in a cross-bow, the fool's wit is
  soon shot (without any thought behind it).
dulcet diseases Soothing discomforts. Some of the remarks may be
  uncomfortable, but they are beneficial.
seeming i.e. properly, appropriately.
in the mind Of the opinion.
disabled i.e. was contemptuous of.
Countercheck Reply contradicting.
Circumstantial On conditions.
durst Dared.
measured words i.e. to check that they are the same length, the
  preliminary to the actual duel, to ensure fairness.
in print, by the book Properly, according to the rules laid down in the
  duelling manual.
swore brothers i.e. took an oath to behave like brothers, an ironic
  comment in the context of this play.
Your If . . . Touchstone's speech is an important analysis of the art of
  compromise, and 'If' is the important qualification, since it delays or
  prevents action.
stalking-horse Literally, this is a horse trained to conceal a hunter's
  approach, so that he can get within easy range of his quarry. The

fool's approach to his target is disguised by jesting.

pressentation Appearance.

Atone Are in agreement.

Hymen The god of marriage.

truth in sight i.e. if my eyes don't deceive me.

If sight and shape be true If my eyes see clearly and your appearance is real.

bar Prohibit.

Hymen's bands i.e. marriage.

truth holds true contents You are satisfied with the truth (now that you have seen it).

cross Disagreement.

Feed Satisfy.

That reason . . . diminish So that the true facts may be explained.

great Juno's crown i.e. the highest reward that the most powerful goddess can confer.

Thy faith . . . Your faithfulness now attracts me to you.

Address'd Directed.

In his own conduct Under his command.

skirts Outskirts.

question Conversation.

from the world i.e. Duke Frederick became a monk.

This to be true I swear to the truth (of what I have just said).

offer'st fairly Bring a welcome present.

potent Powerful.

do those ends Complete what has to be done.

shrewd Sharp.

measure of their states Their ranks and positions.

new-fall'n Just discovered.

measures (a) dance (b) a pun too on 'measure' – the allocation of drink.

put on Taken to.

convertites Who have been converted.

wrangling Bickering, arguing.

loving voyage . . . victuall'd The implication is that Touchstone's marriage to Audrey isn't likely to last long.

other Other things.

Epilogue The closing speech of the play, usually addressed to the audience.

needs no bush Needs no advertisement.

bushes Branches used by wine-merchants to advertise their wines.

case Dilemma.

insinuate Win favour.

furnished Clothed (Rosalind would be in good, perhaps expensive, clothing).

conjure Put a spell on.

complexions that liked me i.e. appearances that I found attractive.

defied not Did not find unpleasant.

curtsy i.e. to the audience.

Revision questions on Act V

1 In what ways do you find the ending of the play satisfactory, and in what ways unsatisfactory?

2 Describe in some detail how Rosalind manages to resolve the various romantic problems in the play.

3 Write on the songs in *As You Like It*, with particular reference to those which are sung in Act V.

4 Describe the part played by Duke Senior, Touchstone and Jaques de Boys in this act.

5 Discuss the use of verse and prose in Act V.

Shakespeare's art in *As You Like It*
Themes

Comedy deals with the lighter aspects of life, and always ends happily, and this romantic comedy has its main themes firmly – but still lightly – centred on love. The love-at-first-sight *motif* occurs in three instances – Rosalind and Orlando, Celia and Oliver, and Phebe and Ganymede/Rosalind. But *As You Like It* has a dark side, for the treachery of brother to brother is duplicated too, and Jaques's satire indicates a world-weariness perhaps not shared by his creator, though it is certainly given full expression. Linked to this darker theme is the contrast which runs throughout between the way of life at court and the way of life in nature, with a sometimes lyrical elevation of nature. (Note, however, that Duke Senior does return to court after his brother has been converted by an old religious man.)

In main outline, then, the themes are clear, and they end with repentance and reconciliation, as in the case of Duke Frederick and Oliver. But they are underpinned by a simple symbolism; Oliver goes to the forest, and finds love and a new life free from envy and his own tyranny. The usurping Duke goes to the forest and finds religion. The good Duke finds that the 'uses of adversity' in nature are 'sweet', and all the lovers find love there – only Touchstone, perhaps, finding lust, and Jaques finding more material for moralizing. The emphasis on reconciliation and repentance is not convincing, but the emphasis on love is, and it is done by way of contrast between the real figures – Rosalind and Orlando – and those of pastoral convention – Silvius and Phebe. In much Elizabethan literature there is an idealization of country life, derived perhaps from the revival of classical learning during the 16th century. There was something escapist about reading stories of shepherds tending their flocks in Arcadia, with no other concerns but those of love. Shakespeare's theme burlesques this through Silvius and Phebe, and also by providing a thematic contrast in real rustics like Audrey, William and Corin. The idea that the lady's indifference means death to the lover – a favourite pastoral theme – is mocked in the character of Silvius and in Rosalind's assertion that man has never died for love. Even in the romantic main plot though, there is some mockery, for Orlando's extravagant versifying and his display of it is also made a butt for satire, as Touchstone demonstrates. It should be added that the love element in the play is enhanced by the major theme of mistaken identity. The themes are love, affected or exaggerated love, unnatural behaviour, contrast between court life and life in nature and, ultimately, reconciliation and repentance.

Setting and atmosphere

Intimately linked to the themes are the setting and atmosphere of the play. Nominally the scene is France – Oliver describes Orlando as 'the stubbornest young fellow of France' – for the forest is that of the Ardennes in north-east France. The time setting does not matter, but we note that Amiens and Le Beau have French names. Shakespeare is undoubtedly using a duality here, for he has in mind that other forest of Arden in his native Warwickshire. The importance of the location is that it is in the open air, away from the court, and to be banished is a means of finding true values against the foreground of nature. There is evil and 'rough weather', but it is resisted and endured. The animal population range from the birds and the deer to a snake and a starving lioness. The result is a feeling of spaciousness and of escape from the ordinary cares of life. It is not the forest of the conventional pastoral or a real English forest, but an imaginary wood of Shakespeare's own making. We cannot even identify the time of year with any certainty, for there is mention of the 'winter's wind', the 'bleak air', but also Touchstone basks in the sun while two of the songs, 'Under the greenwood tree' and 'It was a lover and his lass' surely belong to spring or early summer. Obviously the author's aim was to produce a general picture of outdoor life, but with a symbolic overtone. Thus the references to winter weather reflect the uneasy and unpleasant life at court as mirrored in Duke Frederick and Oliver; but winter weather cannot be as unkind 'as man's ingratitude'. As we said earlier, the move to nature ultimately leads to repentance, reconciliation, love. Man can recover his nature from nature itself, which exists in the natural seasonal extremes, but not in unnatural familial envy or the thrusting ambition of court life.

The characters

Rosalind

Let me see, what think you of falling in love?

Rosalind, with Viola of *Twelfth Night*, is perhaps the most winningly attractive of Shakespeare's heroines. We learn that she is bright, vivacious and happy though we first see her downcast at her father's banishment. She is a brilliant player on words – innuendo, double entendre and puns, all being her stock-in-trade. She can spar verbally with Touchstone, is much the more eloquent in her exchanges with Orlando, and though initially Celia is her equal, Rosalind's experiences in love somehow bring out the resilience of her character. Rosalind is high-born, educated and fluent. She takes the measure of every character she meets, speaking of the sycophantic Le Beau as being 'news-crammed', picking up Touchstone's word 'rank' to retort wittily 'Thou losest thy old smell'. At the beginning of the play she is not embittered though perhaps out of spirits and she quickly forgets her own sufferings in her sympathy for the old man whose sons have been defeated by Charles, and in her concern for Orlando. Rosalind is romantic in a romantic comedy, and consequently she is vulnerable and impressionable despite her commonsense. In fact we sense that she *wants* to see the wrestling simply to distract herself from her depression. But on seeing Orlando, and falling in love with him at first sight, she tries to dissuade him from the bout. She spontaneously gives her chain – all she has to give – to Orlando. She soon confides her love to Celia 'these burs are in my heart' but even here we see her resilience, for she is sexually witty on her own account. Rosalind has to be resilient, for she is banished by Duke Senior, and makes a noble and sincere appeal to him which reveals her inherent quality. She has dignity and truth on her side ('Treason is not inherited, my lord') but she is overcome by the sentence. She rallies quickly in response to Celia's generous spirit. She enters into the challenge of disguise with gusto, saying 'We'll have a swashing and a martial outside' and appropriately chooses Ganymede as her alias. However, her basic insecurity about their venture is revealed when she urges Celia to take Touchstone with them.

Once away from the court and in the forest of Arden Rosalind grows in stature (I choose the word deliberately) since, assuming the man's part, she also has to assume the decisiveness and degree of bravado which must go with it. As she says, 'doublet and hose ought to show itself courageous to petticoat'. But we are never allowed to forget – just as Rosalind never forgets – that she is a woman. Her ready sympathy is at first given to Silvius as he laments for Phebe, but even here she can be witty and self-aware at the same time

Jove, Jove! this shepherd's passion
Is much upon my fashion . . . (Act II Scene 4)

Having found Orlando's verses, she responds to Touchstone's witticisms about them with some harsh language which conceals her own flutter. And when Celia reads some others aloud, Rosalind is able to comment adversely on the scansion! But when Rosalind learns that the author is Orlando her questions are as quick as her heart-beat. Hearing that Orlando is dressed like a hunter, she observes 'he comes to kill my heart'; and when Orlando appears she has the presence of mind to tell Celia 'Slink by and note him.' And here we note one of Rosalind's most fascinating qualities – her ability to improvise, to deceive and yet seize the main chance – that of expressing her love for Orlando obliquely beneath her disguise. Her wit, some of it sexual, overcomes Orlando who, of course, does not recognize her. She displays a capacity for innuendo which is wide ranging in its suggestion – she takes in time, love-sickness in particular, with satirical intent, her target being the conventional appearance of love as distinct from the real feeling. But her own cunning fashions the rules of the game she is playing – that Orlando shall imagine that she is his 'Rosalind' – as indeed she is! This admirable duplicity satisfies her and him in part, and adds a rich level of comedy to the play. Yet it also partakes of pathos, for Rosalind, with all her worldly reference, is still maidenly enough not to reveal who she is. Rosalind also wishes to be wooed just as much as Orlando wishes to woo; as we would say today, the game is for real. The strength of her love and her femininity are shown when she worries about Orlando being late for their meeting, and although she listens to Celia's criticisms she is in no way disloyal to Orlando.

Rosalind's attack on Phebe for her treatment of Silvius is perhaps a reflection of her own insecurity, but the language – remember that she is acting the part of a man – shows what a rounded character Shakespeare has created in this vivacious and here outspoken heroine. Having damned Phebe with a bluntness that is certainly insulting and strongly felt, she tells her 'Down on your knees/And thank heaven, fasting, for a good man's love,' The irony is that she herself cherishes the love of a good man, but because of her position she can only indulge it vicariously. There is a streak of cruelty in her indictment of Phebe, but it is a cruelty born of her own frustration.

She is equal to Jaques's wit, puts him down as a traveller, and waxes satirical about his travels and, by implication, his affectation, including his melancholy. When Orlando does appear she indulges her own fancies – like the comparison with the snail – but is so moved as to be almost cut short in her simple acknowledgement 'And I am your Rosalind'. Deeply moved, she yet has the spirit to inveigh against the popularly held romantic concept that men have died for love. Indeed, she is so adept, so witty, so outspokenly independent in her views and judgements, that we are forced to feel that she is too good for Orlando, who is no match for her wit or spirit. Her analysis of the phases from courtship to marriage and after, which she compares to the seasons as they change, is a superbly cynical pronouncement on what is all too often true. Despite her being in love, she is not inhibited from saying it. She even mocks romantic affected melancholy by cleverly citing her own case – ''Tis but one cast away, and so, come death!' Yet when Orlando has gone, she confesses movingly to Celia just how deeply in love she is. Phebe's letter moves her to more condemnation, since Phebe has been using Silvius as a messenger-dupe, and by reading the letter aloud to him, Silvius finally sees the truth.

Rosalind's fainting at the sight of the bloody napkin shows her essentially feminine nature. She is overcome by the thought that Orlando may be badly hurt. Passingly recovered, she says ironically, ever aware of what she is really, 'I should have been a woman by right'. When she next sees Orlando she covers her counterfeit by concentrating on the sudden love of Celia and Oliver, as sudden but perhaps less convincing than her own, since audience and reader have to accept the reformation of

Oliver. Rosalind's imagination is ever at work, and she invents the story of her own magical powers in order to bring about the wholesale coming together at the end. She takes a delightful, and somewhat lustful, joy in the prospect – 'I will satisfy you, if ever I satisfied man, and you shall be married tomorrow'. With her usual spirit she extracts the necessary promises from the Duke. It is typical of her kindness of heart, her genuineness towards others, that she arranges for the happiness of Silvius as well as her own. Hymen takes over, but even in the epilogue Rosalind's part, though functional, allows her to indulge her wit, saying of men 'for the love you bear to women – as I perceive by your simpering none of you hates them'. Her wit is often at the expense of her own sex, or herself, but she represents among other qualities, integrity. Rosalind is never less than human in all her responses, and her vulnerability, resilience, imagination and sophisticated humour, endear her to us and make her the dominant figure in the play.

Celia

And whereo'ere we went, like Juno's swans,
Still we went coupled and inseparable.

There is a critical tendency to see Celia as a mere foil to Rosalind. This is a total misreading of the early part of the play. Celia is generous, kind, witty, loyal, courageous and sympathetic. Her first important statement in the play reflects her quality, and takes on an ironic flavour in view of what happens:

If my uncle thy banished father had banished thy uncle the Duke my father, so thou hadst still been with me, I could have taught my love to take thy father for mine . . . (Act I Scene 2)

She is soon to be put to the test, but before that she does her utmost to cheer up Rosalind, suggesting that they turn their imaginations towards other things in order to distract Rosalind from her grief at her father's banishment. She debates Fortune, Nature and Love, and greets the arrival of Touchstone with some cutting innuendo and even a threat. But generally she is kind, sympathetic and independent, though the temptation to see the wrestling and the breaking of more ribs is too much for her. She further indulges her wit at the expense of Le Beau, plays on words as skilfully as Rosalind, capping his story wittily before he begins it by observing 'I could match this beginning with an old tale.' She it is who calls Orlando to them before the wrestling – we must remember that she is the present Duke's daughter and commands authority – and adds her concern to the more manifest anxiety of Rosalind. She also wishes 'I would I were invisible, to catch the strong fellow by the leg' (i.e. Charles), an indication of her vivacity and imagination at one and the same time. She is honest and outspoken, saying

Let us go thank him and encourage him.
My father's rough and envious disposition
Sticks me at heart . . . (Act I Scene 2)

It is hardly the remark of a dutiful daughter, and it reveals that quality of unconventional independence and rightness of feeling in Celia that mark her out as an individual in her own right and not the usurped right of her father.

Seeing that Rosalind has fallen in love, she teases her for her silence ('come lame me with reasons') and urges her in appropriate metaphor 'Come, come, wrestle with thy affections.' She has no trace of envy or jealousy in her disposition, and when her father suggests that Rosalind's popularity undermines Celia's position she refuses to heed his words. Her response to her father's banishment is loyal and spiritedly unequivocal, 'If she be traitor/Why so am I', and it is her resourcefulness that leads to their flight. She feelingly offers to change fathers with Rosalind (in a sense, she does so at the end), works out her own disguise for their flight, and rouses in Rosalind a like spirit of challenge. She obviously feels more for the banished Duke 'My uncle' than for her father 'Dear sovereign', another indication of her rightness of heart. Yet there is something pathetic in her choice of name, Aliena, the desolate one, since she is indeed forsaking family for loyalty and love, putting human sympathy and her integrity before position and false familial allegiance. The pathos is further heightened by her jumping at Rosalind's suggestion that they should take Touchstone with them: their mutual devotion ensures that one of her 'family' accompanies her. She is stoic, in no way sorry for herself as illustrated by her climaxing couplet to Act I after she has said that they will be pursued

         Now go we in content
To liberty, and not to banishment. (Act I Scene 3)

She plays a less important part once they arrive in the Forest of Arden. She is obviously not as strong as Rosalind, and is nearly fainting from exhaustion. She soon appreciates the place however, but her role becomes more functional. She finds some of Orlando's verses about Rosalind, and teases the latter, hugely enjoying the joke that Rosalind does not know who wrote them whereas she, Celia, does. She indulges herself in sexual wit at Rosalind's expense, for she too has a sharp mind and enjoys following out an innuendo. Her account of discovering Orlando is endowed with her own wry humour ('I found him under a tree like a dropped acorn') and she follows this with her own small satirical shaft at romantic courtship ('There lay he stretched along like a wounded knight'). She continues to tease Rosalind, answering the latter's questions about whether she thinks Orlando is true in love with some nicely acidic coinages of her own 'But all's brave that youth mounts and folly guides.' She takes part in the mock-marriage ceremony between Rosalind and Orlando, but mocks Rosalind afterwards by telling her that 'You have simply misused our sex in your love-prate'.

When Rosalind is indulging to the full her melancholy, Celia laconically observes 'And I'll sleep'. It is the language of practicality, but soon she is to be caught up in romance herself. She feels pity for Silvius in his love for Phebe, helps Oliver support Ganymede and falls in love with him though this, tellingly, happens off-stage. Ironically, she does not speak another word in the play, and we feel the loss, for Celia is the natural counterpoint to Rosalind. Precise, ever practical and alert, she has a cool head in an emergency, even reminding Rosalind at one stage of her disguise. It is surprising that she takes Oliver's reformation without question, and perhaps Shakespeare is wise to have this reported, for we should certainly need to suspend our disbelief if it were seen, since Celia has earlier warned Rosalind about falling in love quickly, and indeed seems chary of doing so herself. But Celia is essentially likeable, warm, sympathetic and, though less impulsive than Rosalind, quite as susceptible in the end.

Orlando

He's gentle, never schooled, and yet learned;
full of noble device;
of all sorts enchantingly beloved.

Orlando kept down by his older brother tastes the sharpness of adversity. Yet he has the spirit to rebel, and we come to recognize later that it is the spirit of his father. His first speech in the play promises much, for we sense the bitterness and resentment which he feels at his degrading treatment. His violent reaction when he seizes Oliver by the neck indicates his physical strength, but again we are led to expect more than is evidenced by the love-struck youth later in the play.

Prior to the wrestling he conducts himself with modesty and forbearance, but his speech to Rosalind and Celia smacks of pathos – we might unkindly call it self-pity – 'I shall do my friends no wrong, for I have none to lament me.' Yet this in itself is a moving testimony to his deprivation. He responds positively to Charles's mocking, physically by throwing him, and then to the Duke's sullen recognition of him with a true spirit of family pride. He is immediately thrown himself by Rosalind, at least metaphorically, finding 'What passion hangs these weights upon my tongue?', and from then on he becomes a changed character, almost a stereotype of romantic love. He too leaves for the forest, after having been warned by Adam that Oliver is intent upon killing him. Here again he shows his noble quality, refusing to debase his blood by theft or anything degrading. He is deeply touched by Adam's giving him his savings to further their journey, and indicts the times in which he lives. Here we see Orlando as representing goodness in a world which recognizes thrusting ambition and corruption as the measures of success, and this tends to further establish him as a symbolic figure in the moral patterning of the play.

Orlando cares for Adam in their particular adversity, and breaks into Duke Senior's camp in order to get food and succour for the old man. At first threatening, he again reveals his nobility of nature by responding to the gentle welcome he receives, and his speech of recognition to Duke Senior is imbued with religious goodness and spirituality, the practical christianity which is at the heart of the matter here. He says, 'Let gentleness my strong enforcement be', and puts Adam before himself by bringing him to eat and thanking the Duke on his (Adam's) behalf. This food and shelter obtained, he reverts to his love for Rosalind, here representing the extreme of romantic praise and the self-indulgence of romantic verses, which both Celia – genuinely – and Rosalind – perhaps affectedly – recognize as bad. There is something pompous about his exchange with Jaques – 'I pray you mar no more of my verses with reading them ill-favouredly' – but even before the mock-wooing and the mock-marriage Orlando is out-talked and outwitted by Rosalind as Ganymede. He readily agrees to the wooing, and finds himself on the receiving end of much wit and wisdom from Rosalind. There is an unevenness about this which is somewhat distasteful; we must wonder whether Rosalind won't find him a rather dull companion after marriage. His rescue of Oliver clinches his essential nobility.

Although he gives his consent willingly to Oliver's marriage to Celia, he finds it hard to believe that they met and fell in love at first sight, though he himself has done just that in the past. He bemoans his own fate in not being married when Celia and Oliver are, but it is Rosalind who shows the initiative, not Orlando. Yet at the back of his mind he admits that Ganymede bears some resemblance to the Duke's daughter i.e. Rosalind. Orlando is always so much in love that all he really wants to do is to talk of his Rosalind, for it is the only form of self-indulgence left to him.

Brave, handsome, strong physically, noble in nature, gentle in intention and sympathy, he is good in outline but, unlike his bride, he is not fully developed enough to be convincing. Perhaps his finest quality should be given some stress though; he is not prepared to blame the world. He rather blames himself for what occurs, and his romantic melancholy is not based on affectation but on a genuine depression.

Oliver

And well he might do so,
For well I know he was unnatural

Oliver's words about himself unfortunately strike an unnatural note too, but since one of the themes of the play is reconciliation and repentance Oliver, like Duke Frederick, must be made to subserve it. He behaves unnaturally over a period of time – unspecified – to Orlando, being vicious and unprincipled. When Orlando stands up to him, Oliver plots to have him killed by Charles the wrestler. He dupes the latter by giving him a false report of Orlando, and thus illustrates how jealous he is of him because of his popularity with the people and his inherent nobility of character. When his attempt to kill Orlando fails, he plans another one. If he is larger than life as a villain, he is smaller than life as a reformed character, and it is this which indicates his functional rather than real role in the moral ethos of the play. Sent away by the Duke to seek Orlando, he goes to the forest without encountering anyone until he is rescued by his natural brother from a starving lioness. His reporting this to Rosalind and Celia is accompanied by his falling in love with Celia at first sight. He seeks his brother's blessing on their union, in repayment for which he will bequeath all his estates to him.

Oliver decides 'to live and die a shepherd', but we can't accept this, and we cannot think that Celia, who has no word to say of her love, would meekly countenance this. His conversion is unconvincing, and we have to turn back to the first scene of the play to see just how unlikely it would be that this inordinate, greedy, jealous and unscrupulous young man would change. He does; but it fits the ideal structure of the play, not the reality of living. He parallels Duke Frederick at every count.

Touchstone

He uses his folly like a stalking-horse,
and under the presentation of that he shoots his wit.

Touchstone is called both clown and fool, once 'clownish fool'. Interestingly, in the stage directions to the First Folio he is generally 'Clowne' and once 'Clowne alias Touchstone'. He is a professional, a jester employed at the court, and thus his business is with words. He wears the parti-coloured motley fitting for his position, which Jaques affects he would like to appropriate himself. The court jester had to be clever, witty and keep himself on the right side of his employers. He was allowed much freedom of expression ('there is no licence in an allowed fool', says Olivia in *Twelfth Night*) but Touchstone is no fool in the simple sense of the word, nor is he motley-minded, as Jaques would have us believe. But that freedom has its limits, and Celia warns him 'You'll be whipped for taxation (satire, ridicule) one of these days.' Fortunately, the threat does not inhibit Touchstone. He is the master of word-play, as he demonstrates on his first entrance, and he is master too of proverbial wisdom 'The more pity that fools may not speak wisely what wisemen do foolishly' (Act I Scene 2). He enters into the baiting of Le Beau, though he is himself crossed by Rosalind and Celia. His devotion to Celia leads him to accompany both girls into the forest where he seeks out his own company (in the form of Audrey) doubtless with an eye to sexual satisfaction. He enjoys his new role of condescension to the rustic wench, and his own ability to utter what she cannot possibly understand. He enjoys duping and threatening, as with Audrey and William. But at the same time Touchstone is able to wax satirical about love in a comedy which embodies romantic love as its major theme. As he observes, 'We that are true lovers run into stranger capers; but as all is mortal in nature, so is all nature in love mortal in folly' (Act II Scene 4). Touchstone is ever-adept at the pun (only Rosalind can match him here) and in some ways his satirical bent and his cynicism – though not his temperament – correspond to that of Jaques. Touchstone's wit at the expense of love and marriage even embraces a brilliant parody of Orlando's verses on Rosalind, with a salacious sexual innuendo which reflects his own designs on Audrey:

Winter'd garments must be lin'd,
So must slender Rosalind.
They that reap must sheaf and bind,
Then to cart with Rosalind . . . (Act III Scene 2)

His affair with Audrey (with the cruel streak of his treatment of William) is a burlesque of love, and is obviously used in the structure of the play to contrast with the romantic love of Rosalind and Orlando. He is an opportunist, employing Sir Oliver Martext to conduct a 'mock' marriage ceremony so that he may 'have' Audrey without any legal repercussions. He ridicules courtiers and the manners of the court on a number of occasions, notably in his discussion with Corin in Act III Scene 2, and in the telling of his own experiences as a courtier to the Duke and Jaques in Act V Scene 4. Touchstone is the master of rhetoric, and, since he lives by playing with words, this is extended and qualified, as in his threats to the uncomprehending William in Act V Scene 2. His introduction of his bride-to-be Audrey to the Duke in Act V Scene 4 continues the burlesque strain, with his references to 'country copulatives' and 'marriage binds and blood breaks'. His command of innuendo and mockery perhaps reaches its highest point in the 'lie seven times removed' exchanges with Jaques. This again has an important part in the structure of the play, for there is little doubt that the duelling innuendo is a burlesque of Jaques's seven ages of man speech (which Touchstone has not heard). It is a sustained satire on the code of duelling, couched in verbal and fighting terms. The elaborate terms mock courtly behaviour and repartee as do the nonsensical roundabout exchanges which mark off court life from reality. Elsewhere there is evidence that Jaques's moralizing finds its echo in Touchstone's. The final quip of the speech 'Your If is the only peacemaker: much virtue in If' spells out the way in which cowardice can be resolved by compromise, quarrel by indecision, loss of face by that qualifying small word which excuses all. Jaques rightly describes Touchstone as a 'material fool', and perhaps envies him the freedom he has to expose the follies of his fellow men in his paid professional role.

Jaques

> But what said Jaques?
> Did he not moralize this spectacle?

Jaques is known to everyone for his affectation of melancholy, or perhaps it is that it has become so much part of him he wears it naturally instead of the motley he craves. It is somewhat ironic that he has the finest speech in the play, for 'All the world's a stage' is not merely the most quoted speech in Shakespeare, it is a piece of moralizing which has a timeless truth. It *focusses* on the seven wonders of the world reducing them to the seven phases of existence from the cradle to the grave. Here, with the theatre analogy central to it, Jaques may be his author's mouthpiece, but it seems unlikely that he is elsewhere. Jaques delights – if that isn't too strong a word – in his own melancholy, and looks for the opportunity to moralize – to draw philosophical conclusions in his case – on everything he sees. There is little doubt that he represents disillusionment with life, but this may be explained by the fact that, as the Duke reveals, he was given to wild behaviour in his youth. The theme of repentance, however, does not touch him. He boasts to Rosalind of his travels, saying how they have contributed to the 'melancholy of mine own, compounded of many simples, extracted from many objects', and there is also little doubt that he provides food for amusement for his companions.

Jaques is something of a prig, holding love cheaply, and a

poseur, intent on displaying the mark of his difference from others. He sees the worst aspects of life and regales others with his views of those aspects, presenting pessimism as the natural creed for all to embrace. He may see the world as a theatre, but for him life is certainly a miserable performance. It is mean and petty, and he is able to pronounce on its vanity, all natural behaviour and creatures in nature, like the dying stag, being grist to his melancholy mill. We understand his pleasure in Touchstone, whose motley – official – makes him both a parody of a man and the parodist of man. Jaques himself does however see into the corruptions of the court, and finds them reflected in nature too. Weary and affected, he needs the constant stimulus of distraction to supply him with material, hence his interest in the conversion of the usurping Duke Frederick. He is, to use his own words, always for 'other measures', and Touchstone by chance provides them, for the latter's first overheard monologue on Time strikes a chord in the responsive Jaques. Thereafter Jaques delights in reporting him, following him, and finally introducing him to Duke Senior, perhaps in the hope that the latter will employ him and thus provide Jaques with an ever-present diversion. He manages to get into conversation with Orlando and urges him to rail against 'our mistress the world', but Orlando is more interested in his own mistress. Jaques even introduces himself to Rosalind (she is disguised of course as Ganymede) but gets little moralizing change out of her. His final movement towards Duke Frederick shows at least that he practises what he preaches, for he is turning his back on the court.

Jaques seems out of place in the forest, for although he can indulge his sentimentality to the full over the stag, he is really making the incident an excuse for his own world-weary, indolent philosophy, his dislike of the life of the exiled court. Thus he parodies Amiens's beautiful song 'Under the Greenwood Tree', his 'Ducdame' refrain sufficiently indicative of his contempt both for the song and the life. He makes an excellent contrast to the other characters of the play, whether real, romantic, or evil until repentant. The fact is that he has opted out of life into reflection, living vicariously by words alone. In this sense there is an air of pathos and loneliness about him which critics have tended to ignore.

Jaques is not part of the action, for he is an observer not a doer, and in plays as in life the doers register with the watchers and listeners. He is self-centred, self-opinionated, in short complacent in a cynical and detached way despite his own interest in the doings of others. We may admire his main great speech, and indeed his command of words, but in the end he represents affectation rather than reality – with perhaps the subtle innuendo from his creator that many people represent just that too.

Duke Senior

Sweet are the uses of adversity

The line quoted above is the key to the Duke's somewhat idealized character, which is obviously meant to stand in contrast to that of Duke Frederick. He is good-natured, tolerant, making the best of the natural life though comparing it tellingly to court life as well in some fine imagery (the stags as 'burghers'). In fact he idealizes a way of life which, later, he is prepared to leave as soon as Fortune smiles on him. Perhaps here Shakespeare is commenting on the nature of human nature. Duke Senior is good-humoured and contented, liking the company of Jaques because he is amused by his affectation. He is gentle, and this is seen markedly on two occasions. The first is when we note that killing deer irks him because he is compelled to do it though he regards them as 'poor dappled fools', living natives of this 'desert city'. The second is his kind reception of the desperate Orlando, for he remains calm, and, when he has heard Orlando's story treats him – and Adam – with kindness and gives them food. He has a very firm sense of humour, and soon becomes friends with Orlando not merely because of his condition but because he respected his father, who had honoured him in better ways. He is clear-sighted too, saying of Touchstone 'By my faith, he is very swift and sententious', which is perhaps a better epitaph than any reader could have coined. Again he receives Jaques de Boys's all-important news calmly and virtually without comment, but considerately promising all his adherents a share in his returned fortunes. He is essential to the theme of injured goodness which undergoes just restoration in *As You Like It*.

Duke Frederick

My father's rough and envious disposition.

Celia's words are an appropriate comment on the Duke Frederick who has usurped his brother Duke Senior. However, in fairness it must be said that he tries to dissuade Orlando from wrestling, and is genuinely sorry when he learns who his father was, a sometime enemy of his own. His 'humorous' disposition means that he is prepared to set aside his daughter's love for Rosalind, and banishes her for in effect being her father's daughter! He also has the insensitivity to tell Celia that Rosalind has usurped her (Celia's) position, and seems unmindful of Celia's emotional identification with Rosalind in her banishment. He is also harsh to Oliver, ordering him to find Orlando, but we can hardly condemn an action against Oliver's own tyranny. Duke Frederick is merely a structural device, for when Jaques de Boys brings the news of his conversion (he had been heading an army intent on capturing and killing his brother Duke Senior) we realize that he is merely a sketch. The improbability of his final action is unconvincing – it merely subserves the theme of repentance.

Adam

O good old man

Adam is the ancient retainer idealized almost beyond belief. His love for Sir Rowland, father of Oliver and Orlando, means that he works towards their reconciliation to no effect. He has the pathos of old age yet, until the long journey to the forest, is hale and hearty enough because of his abstemious life. He has previously warned Orlando of Oliver's intention to burn him alive in his dwelling, and provides his life savings to support them when they leave. This loyalty to the family is the cornerstone of his actions, and in fact he suffers greatly, but is saved and succoured when Orlando finds the camp of Duke Senior.

Silvius and Phebe

Sweet Phebe do not scorn me, do not Phebe.

. . .

Now I do frown on thee with all my heart

These conventional pastoral figures do not appear until Act III
Scene 5, and again we feel that their presence is part of the
structural patterning of the play. His exaggerated sentimentality
and her cruel disdain are part of the pastoral convention, but
through the comments of Rosalind (i.e. on Phebe's 'leather
hand') Shakespeare is able successfully to burlesque the convention. Thus they are caricatures, always speaking in verse in order
to convey the extremes of feeling which they represent.
Although their love-rejection interaction is perfectly serious for
them, the extravagance of their language contrasts with that of
Audrey on the one hand and the romantic lovers Rosalind and
Orlando on the other. Silvius is what Rosalind calls a 'tame
snake', while Phebe, who underpins the love-at-first-sight theme,
has duplicity enough to despatch Corin with her love letter to
Rosalind. Both, but particularly Phebe, come in for the best of
Rosalind's invective. Phebe, to her credit, agrees to abide by
Rosalind's rules with regard to love and marriage. She begins to
see in her rejected love something of the nature of Silvius's
suffering. Both represent artificiality, and their presence in the
play is evidence of Shakespeare's structural artifice. They don't
breathe air, they breathe sentiments.

Corin, Audrey, William

Sir, I am a true labourer
. . .

(Bear your body more seeming, Audrey.)
. . .

'God rest you, merry sir.'

These are three real English country characters, for although
Corin has a conventional pastoral name, he is a working man,
helps Rosalind and Celia to find a 'cote', and has a very homely
philosophy. He has largely forgotten about love, and is really
only concerned about sheep, though we suspect that he is fed up
with another kind of bleating, that of Silvius. He is unimpressed
by Touchstone's courtly wit.

    Audrey is a dim-witted country girl who admires but does not understand Touchstone's wit, thinking that he must be brilliant merely because she can't understand him. She is aware of her own plainness, and flattered at the prospect of marriage (not understanding that it may be faked) to a courtier. She cannot read Touchstone's mind or more particularly his lust, and of course does not comprehend his insults. She evokes little sympathy; Jaques observes that her marriage to Touchstone will probably not last. She would have been better off with *William,* who is no match for Touchstone. He is simple and bewildered. It is not so much that he is bullied into retreat but rather that he does not understand the language used by Touchstone, and can only withdraw from its clamour out of simple rustic politeness.

Structure

The main elements in the structure of *As You Like It* are straight-forward, and will have been obvious from the summary of the plot (see p.12). The time-scale of the action is about ten days, with a few intervals, the duration of which are not indicated and cannot be considered important. The main focus is on the banishment, the fleeing of Orlando, and the certainty that Arden is to be the centre of the action, the dramatic climax of the play occurring in Act III Scene 2, when Orlando meets Rosalind in the forest and the mock-wooing beings. This main plot element has a surround – the actions of the two Dukes and, of course, the earlier brutality and the later repentance of Oliver. We thus see, in the course of the play, the inception, development and conclusion of the main love-story, that of Rosalind and Orlando with the attendant stories of Celia and Oliver (off stage), Touchstone and Audrey, and later Silvius and Phebe. In effect, as this is completed, the two Dukes change places, Duke Senior returning to court to his rightful position (though he has been educated by 'adversity' in nature) and Duke Frederick embracing the religious life (and thus the education of spirit and spirituality). It must be said that after Act I Rosalind is the central character in the play, and most of the action is initiated by her.

The three sub-plots have already been touched upon, and they demonstrate Shakespeare's deliberate use of parallelism and contrast in his structure. Indeed, these are the main elements of it. There are obvious weaknesses. The Silvius/Phebe plot is a counterbalance to the Rosalind/Orlando plot, though there is little dramatic effectiveness in it. It does, however, contribute to the satire of the pastoral convention, providing Rosalind with an opportunity to berate Phebe's disdain. It also contributes to the mistaken identity theme and has a certain degree of pathos in the character of Silvius.

On another level, however, the structure works splendidly, as with the neat satirical balance achieved between Jaques on the one hand and Touchstone on the other. In a sense, too, the main plot is thrown into greater relief by the sub-plots and their parallels and contrasts. All of course contribute to the main theme of love in the play. Above all there is a distinct parallelism in the circumstances and fortunes of Rosalind and Orlando; they are both forced to flee from the malice of evil relations, both are hated by Duke Frederick because of his hatred for their respective fathers, and both take refuge in the forest of Arden accompanied by faithful friend/servant.

The structure of the play allows for the grossest improbabilities, but this should not inhibit our enjoyment. Apart from those referred to above, consider the fact that Rosalind is allowed to remain at court by the 'humorous' Duke after he has banished her father. Once in the forest of Arden she does not immediately seek out her father, as we should expect; Orlando does not recognize her in her masculine disguise, Oliver suddenly changes his character and Celia accepts him with the full knowledge of his past record, and Duke Frederick changes from tyrant to religious hermit. But a play is a structure in itself. The balance throughout is on love, loyalty, tyranny, evil and then reconciliation, all against the background of nature, which is essential to the structure. For the seasons move in extremes, and so does man, and this makes *As You Like It* a coherent whole.

The songs

In *As You Like It* there are seven songs, and it would be true to say that they all have a particular relevance to the structure of the play, while three of them, in addition to being an ironic comment on the main action, have a particular beauty and lyrical quality of their own. The first, sung by Amiens in Act II Scene 5, provides an echo of the Duke's sentiments in praise of nature at the opening of the second act. The praise of nature is at the expense of the court, and the enemy and weather imagery, the mention of ambition, the emphatic refrain, all idealize the natural life and are therefore important to our understanding of the moral element of the play which uses man's corruption and power on the one hand, and the forsaking of it on the other. 'pleas'd with what he gets' is a fine line which is a comment on those who covet more than they should have. Jaques's parody, which immediately follows this, is also effective; it indicates his cynicism, and is a compression of his own moralizing. We see from this brief note on two of the songs that they are integral. Probably they were written with definite airs in mind, and musicians would accompany the singers, but here the obvious purpose is to underline the themes of the play against the appropriate natural background, which is thus given emphasis. 'Blow, blow thou winter wind' is particularly poignant coming, as it does, after Orlando brings Adam to the Duke's table. It covers his explanation – which the audience already knows of – but the comments on friendship and ingratitude are yet another indictment of the court as against nature where the seasons follow each other naturally. The contrast is with the unnatural actions of men, like those of brother against brother. Touchstone's snatch of song in Act III Scene 2 is a popular one of the day and has little relevance to the main themes, except that it signals the end of his 'marriage' venture temporarily. Jaques's song in Act IV Scene 2 again exemplifies his cynicism, with its play on the killing of the deer and the horns of the cuckold, a 'burden' which every man must bear. 'It was a lover and his lass' lyrically celebrates, and perpetuates through its music, the springtime of love. It also exists on another level, that of an effectively simple parody of silly songs about lovers – it has in fact been called silly – but it seems to this writer that it prepares the way for the climactic celebrations which are about to happen. The song in praise of Hymen and marriage is fitting but undistinguished, its six lines celebratory but nothing more. The songs are therefore various in terms of their effect, but at least three are fine lyrics and very evidently part of the overall structure of *As You Like It*.

Style

The style of the play subserves the structure, that is, it consists of parallel and contrast, a kind of antithetical balance being present throughout. The usual division of verse and prose in a Shakespeare play, between the noble characters (who use verse) and the lower (who use prose) is not consistently applied in *As You Like It*. The main areas are defined below.

Verse

There are many rich quotations from *As You Like It*, and verse is employed at particular moments in the action. For example, Rosalind's banishment from the court, the interaction between her and Duke Frederick and Celia, is in the blank verse iambic pentameter characteristic of Shakespeare's plays. The moment here is one of high drama, hence the movement into verse, but prior to that we have Orlando's victory over Charles similarly distinguished. Le Beau as a courtier also speaks in verse, but a character such as Duke Senior is inevitably given verse, perhaps not just because he is a noble but because his sentiments and his character are too. His first speech in Act II is a good example of Shakespeare's use of the unusual and unexpected, the combination of associations which are both imaginative and which enrich the reader's experience:

Sweet are the uses of adversity,
Which like the toad ugly and venomous,
Wears yet a precious jewel in his head;
And this our life, exempt from public haunt,
Finds tongues in trees, books in the running brooks,
Sermons in stones, and good in everything.

Note that the last phrase virtually epitomizes the optimistic conclusion of the play and much of its matter. Jaques's moralizing is put into blank verse, sometimes for satirical reasons (a kind of poetic affectation) and sometimes again for the sheer elevation of what he says. His 'All the world's a stage' may have a deliberately contemporary association, but its timelessness would be diminished if it were in prose. In Act II Scene 3 Adam and Orlando talk in verse, but then the sacrifice of the old man and Orlando's response are sufficient indications of nobility. Corin, Silvius and Phebe, characters within the pastoral convention referred to earlier, naturally talk in somewhat exaggerated blank verse, but this is part of Shakespeare's satirical/ironic intention. Orlando's blank verse to Duke Senior underpins the theme of goodness, giving it a religious quality (Act II Scene 7), but one of the main qualities of *As You Like It* is the use of rhymed as well as unrhymed verse.

We have referred earlier to the songs, but the musical element in *As You Like It* is not confined to them. The rhymed verse extends it, and allows for the exaggerations of romantic love. For example, Orlando hanging his verses on a tree speaks ten lines of poetry, the first eight with alternate lines rhyming, the whole climaxed by a rhyming couplet (Act III Scene 2). In the same scene Rosalind reads some of these verses aloud, and Touchstone executes an impromptu parody of them; both are in octosyllabic couplets, every word rhyming with 'Rosalind'. But just to show that Orlando's love is not limited to one poetic form, we find that Celia reads another of his offerings, generally octosyllabic, but here with alternate lines rhyming. No doubt the intention of Shakespeare is to be satirical, but all three forms demonstrate the nature of his variety and control. Rosalind occasionally uses rhyme herself, for her brilliant 'you are not for all markets' speech (Act III, Scene 5) is followed by another which has the climactic couplet:

And be not proud; though all the world could see,
None could be so abus'd in sight as he.

Phebe's letter to Rosalind maintains the rhyming octosyllabic couplet form, and there is a nice contrast here when Oliver enters almost immediately after Rosalind has read it; reformed, he too is elevated into blank verse, not the strained and studied artificiality of Phebe's, but the natural unforced flow of concern and confession. A further variant use of verse in the play is Hymen's address, and as befits the god of marriage he has a variety of form, beginning with an eight line verse, followed by a six, and then a run of octosyllabic couplets as he addresses the various 'copulatives' in turn. Perhaps we should note the vividness and variety of the poetic imagery used, and also the typical Renaissance fondness for classical allusion.

Prose

This is predominant in *As You Like It,* probably because there are so many humorous scenes. So much of the play depends on sharpness and repartee, particularly in Rosalind and Touch-stone, and this would lose much of its force if it were confined to the blank verse line. Touchstone always speaks in prose (he is, after all, a professional jester without the elevation of his employers), and this allows free punning and wordplay, as in 'For my part, I had rather bear with you than bear you; yet I should bear no cross if I did bear you, for I think you have no money in your purse' (Act II Scene 4). Prose is obviously suitable for witty conversational dialogue, and for scenes lacking in dramatic tension, but Shakespeare's use of it extends beyond this. By a curious irony, although the Duke speaks in verse, as we have seen, characters who do not find adversity sweet speak in prose. Thus Orlando in the opening scene of the play speaks bitterly of his brother's treatment of him in prose; in the following exchange Oliver and Charles – the former plotting the overthrow of Orlando with him – are both given prose, the one because he is 'low' in intentions, the other because of his status. The next scene has Rosalind in adversity – she is depressed because her father has been banished – and the third scene has her reaction to falling in love also in prose. Banished herself, she rises with dignity into verse, as does Celia. Now it is possible that one could ascribe reasons for these changes, but there appears to be a lack of consistency here, since Jaques, who has perhaps the finest poetry in the play, also speaks in prose (witness Act II Scene 5). In this instance it would appear that when Jaques's sentiments partake of what is elevated and not merely satirical, or when they are so affected as to be mocked, they are in verse. But this would be a dangerous generalization. Orlando and Adam, exhausted, speak in prose, appropriate in view of their physical state.

Naturally the lower order characters like Audrey and William speak in prose, as they always do in Shakespeare, but Corin, who is an ordinary labouring man, speaks with equal facility in both verse and prose. Perhaps we should add this. Dramatic prose must be natural and striking when spoken rapidly as in conversation, and Shakespeare in *As You Like It* seems to be employing prose as most appropriate to his themes and to his characters in their private capacities. There is much punning and juggling with words, particularly by Touchstone, Rosalind and the early Celia, and to a certain extent with Jaques, but in *As You Like It* the division between prose and verse, used by upper and lower orders of characters, is not clear-cut. The use of prose seems to depend on mood and atmosphere, and it in no way diminishes the vivid variety of language and imagery which characterizes the play.

Dramatic irony

Strictly speaking, dramatic irony is not a part of style, but I have included it in this section because it is part of the style of the play in conception rather than in verbal terms. The basis of dramatic irony is ambiguity; a remark may have one meaning for the characters on stage, but a different meaning for the audience. This kind of ambiguity is used in *As You Like It* for both comic and pathetic effect. Thus the double meaning in, for example, Orlando's 'Fair youth, I would I could make thee believe I love' is answered by Rosalind's 'Me believe it! you may as soon make her that you love believe it'. When she tells Celia of her meeting with Duke Senior (who is her father) she says 'He asked me what parentage I was; I told him, of as good as he'. When Phebe obviously falls in love with Rosalind at first sight, the latter tries to warn her off:

I pray you do not fall in love with me,
For I am falser than vows made in wine.

The verbal play in each case reinforces the joke, whether it be pathetic, romantic or self-mocking. But when Rosalind swoons, or counterfeits, as she puts it, the audience knows that she is woman and that the swoon is real because of her love for Orlando. This is non-verbal dramatic irony, the irony of situation which runs throughout the play. For example, the whole of the sequence in which Rosalind is intent on letting all the characters know that she will put things right because she has been trained by a magician, is richly ironic. The audience knows that she only has to reveal herself as a woman to show Orlando his Rosalind, cure Phebe of her love, and reveal his daughter to her own father. From the moment that Rosalind assumes her disguise as Ganymede the humour of the play is largely dependent on the dramatic irony of the audience knowing what most of the characters do not know, namely that Rosalind is a woman.

General questions

1 Indicate by close reference to the play the part taken by Celia in *As You Like It*.

Note guidelines

(a) *Introduction* – who Celia is, her father, the court position. (b) *Early impressions* – attempts to cheer up Rosalind – concern for her friend – quality of her humour and imagination – quickness of wit – exchange with Touchstone – reception of Le Beau – attitude towards wrestling (and Orlando) – concern on Orlando's account – teasing of Rosalind (but good-natured) – loyalty to Rosalind – practicality – plans journey – chooses Aliena as name. (c) *On arrival in forest* – begins to play subsidiary part to Rosalind – likes the forest – appearances in action less frequent – reads Orlando's verses – teases Rosalind again – wit now in evidence again – reveals that it is Orlando who is pinning verses to Rosalind on the trees – humouring of Rosalind about her love – playful, mocking – 'marries' Ganymede and Orlando – mocks Rosalind afterwards – pities Silvius – helps Oliver to look after Rosalind after the swoon – reported fallen in love with Oliver – marries him (end of Act V) – does not speak in final act. (d) *Conclusion* – represents loyalty in friendship, wit, spirit, sympathy etc – influence for good – but fades from action – why would she accept Oliver? – just a structural necessity to round off things given her positive characteristics earlier on. From Rosalind's equal to subsidiary – perhaps Rosalind developed at her expense.

2 Do you consider that the sub-plot of Touchstone and Audrey contributes to our appreciation of the main plot? Give reasons for your answer.

3 Consider the roles played by Duke Frederick and Oliver in the plot. How far do you find them convincing?

4 Discuss the inconsistencies and improbabilities of *As You Like It*. How far do they affect your response to the play?

5 By close reference to the play, show how we are kept aware of the contrast between the corrupt life of the court and the free and honest life of the forest.

6 Compare and contrast Touchstone and Jaques, with particular attention to their satirical wit.

7 Why is *As You Like It* described as a 'romantic comedy'?

8 What use does Shakespeare make of the pastoral characters and the natural background in the play?

9 Love at first sight is the major theme of this comedy. Compare and contrast the various love affairs in the play.

10 Show how the qualities of Rosalind's character throw into relief the follies and weaknesses of other characters in the play.

11 What are the main attractions in Rosalind's character for you as the reader? Refer closely to the text in your answer.

12 Is Orlando a convincing character? How far do you think he is worthy of Rosalind?

13 Write an essay on wit and word-play in *As You Like It*.

14 In what ways does their presence in the forest of Arden influence the characters in *As You Like It*?

15 Write an essay on Shakespeare's use of (a) blank verse (b) rhyming verse and (c) prose in *As You Like It*.

16 Discuss the use of dramatic irony in this play *or* the use of song.

17 Compare and contrast any two characters not mentioned in the questions above.

18 'There is a dark side to *As You Like It*.' Discuss.

19 Analyse the effects of mistaken identity in *As You Like It*.

20 Write an appreciation of Jaques's 'All the world's a stage' speech, indicating clearly what comments you think he is making on the nature of life.

Further reading

The Arden Shakespeare: As You Like It, edited by Agnes Latham (Methuen 1975). Read particularly the critical sections of the Introduction.

Shakespearian Comedy, H. B. Charlton (University Paperbacks, Methuen 1966)

An Approach to Shakespeare, D. A. Traversi (Hollis and Carter 1968)